SUPER FOOD RECIPE BOOK

Sensational Smoothies,
Delicious Dinners, and Guilt-Free
Sweets for a Brand New You

Lynn & Reno Rollé

Foreword by Michelin®-Starred Chef Magnus Hansson

Dedication and Acknowledgments

We dedicate this book to our children, Reno Jr. and Ryann, who inspire us each day to make the world a better place. Without you, Reno Jr., and your struggles as a young boy, we may never have discovered the true healing power of super foods.

Special thanks to Keira Geary for her tireless effort in helping to create this book. You have been an invaluable member of the BōKU team with your infectious smile, beautiful soul, and amazing attitude!

Castle Point Publishing

58 Ninth Street

Hoboken, NJ 07030

Cover design by Susan Livingston

ISBN: 978-0-692-62707-5

Printed and bound in the United States of America

2 4 6 8 10 9 7 5 4 3 1

Contents

Foreword

As a chef who has dedicated his life to creating meals that are both delicious and nutritious, I'm always exploring ways to introduce the world's most potent superfoods into my recipes. That's why I was so was intrigued by BōKU Super Foods when I first read about them online! All of their products are formulated by a naturopathic doctor and lead the industry in purity standards. Not only were the ingredients the most pristine available, but they were formulated in combinations that were completely unique.

When I reached out to BōKU directly, I was delighted to meet Lynn and Reno Rollé, its founders. Their passion for their product and commitment to quality was evident from the first time I spoke to them. It was also evident the first time I tasted BōKU's products myself! There are countless companies claiming to offer great superfoods—I have tried most, if not all, of them. But once I began experimenting with the BōKU lineup, I knew right away that I had discovered my favorite superfood products! In my opinion, there is nothing on the market that even comes close.

I've always been a passionate advocate of organic superfoods, but BōKU makes it even easier. Not only do these amazing gifts from nature increase your health, they taste delicious! That's what this great new cookbook from Lynn and Reno is all about. Have fun and put these exciting recipes to the test! Thanks to BōKU, you will soon discover (as I have) that eating the most nutrient-dense foods on Earth can be incredibly tasty, too!

Magnus Hansson

Key to Icons

Antioxidants

Protein

Detox

Super Food

Energy

Shaker

Immunity

Introduction

Our story, sadly, is one that a lot of families can probably relate to. In 1994, our son was diagnosed with a focus problem. The doctor decided that he needed mind-altering pharmaceuticals to "calm him down" and give him a more "normal life." Shocked by this automatic prescription-writing, we immediately began searching for natural, less harmful alternatives. We were not going to give up without a fight! We began to learn that nutrition plays a huge role in our health and wellness, and we were led to a naturopathic physician who had experienced recent success using blue-green algae, spirulina, and other potent, live foods to achieve incredible health benefits.

In the following years, we sampled and familiarized ourselves with various ingredients from all over the world. It was an amazing journey, one that allowed us to work with some of the most gifted minds in nutritional science. The results are our Super Food Blends, which use only the most pristine, nutrient-dense, healthy ingredients in the world, obtained from fair-trade and sustainable sources whenever possible. They're kosher, vegan, and USDA-certified organic; completely free of GMOs; and contain no nasty fillers of any kind, including gluten, soy, or dairy. Only the good stuff!

Since we're committed to providing our valued customers with the absolute highest quality, most delicious superfood products available anywhere on Earth, we also wanted to provide you with high-quality, delicious recipes to prepare with them! These easy-to-make recipes not only reward your body with the enriching, straight-from-the-earth nutrients packed into every BōKU product, but they delight your taste buds with special twists on classic dishes. Inside you'll find recipes for smoothies; hot drinks and other super sips; snacks and dips; soups, salads, and sides; lunches and dinners; and last but not least, healthy desserts. We hope you enjoy them as much as we've enjoyed bringing them to you!

Merci BōKU,
Lynn and Reno Rollé

Smoothies

Green and Lean Smoothie

This is the ultimate green smoothie. In addition to the variety of vitamin-, mineral- and nutrient-rich fresh vegetables the smoothie contains, the BōKU Super Food powder blend boasts super greens (land, aquatic, and grasses), super fruits, functional mushrooms, super sprouts, vitamins, antioxidants, and enzymes. Plus, the chia seeds and avocado feed your body with the healthy fats and omega-3 it wants, as well as with vitamins A, B, C, E, and K; copper; iron; phosphorous; magnesium; and potassium!

Prep time: 3 minutes   **Serves:** 1

- 1–1½ cups ice
- 1 tablespoon (1 scoop) BōKU Super Food
- 1 banana
- 1 kale leaf
- 8 spinach leaves
- 1 stalk celery
- ½ small avocado
- 1 teaspoon chia seeds
- 2 tablespoons raisins
- 2 tablespoons cashews
- ½ cup coconut milk
- ½ cup rice milk

How to BōKU
Add all ingredients to a high-powered blender. Blend until smooth and creamy.

Fruity Veggie Smoothie

Big leafy greens aren't just for salads anymore. Put away your salad bowl, grab your blender, and prepare to be pleasantly surprised. By using mild-flavored greens and naturally sweet fruit, it's easy and delicious to consume your daily greens. With the combination of BōKU Super Food and fibrous leafy greens in this concoction, you'll feel the unstoppable difference that "going green" can make!

Prep time: 3 minutes   **Serves:** 1

> 1 banana
>
> 1 cup your favorite frozen fruit (such as strawberries or mixed berries)
>
> 3 big leaves anything dark, green, and leafy (spinach, Swiss chard, amaranth), cut into medium pieces
>
> 1 tablespoon (1 scoop) BōKU Super Food
>
> Almond milk or ice (optional)

How to BōKU

Blend all ingredients in a high-powered blender until smooth. To adjust consistency, blend in ice for a thicker smoothie or almond milk for a thinner one.

BōKU Go-To Kale Smoothie

The **BōKU Go-To Kale Smoothie** is a "green" variation of the traditional piña colada. With BōKU Super Food as the star of the show, this smoothie boasts super greens (land, aquatic, and grasses), super fruits, functional mushrooms, super sprouts, vitamins, antioxidants, and enzymes. Kale provides calcium, fiber and manganese, while mango adds vitamins, antioxidants, fiber, and digestive enzymes. Last but certainly not least, cashew—a low-fat, protein-dense, and mineral-rich nut—gives the smoothie a smooth, creamy finish.

Prep time: 3 minutes   **Serves:** 1

   1 banana

   1 tablespoon coconut oil

   2 dates, pitted

   ½ cup pineapple juice

   ½ cup mango

   1 tablespoon cashews

   2 leaves dinosaur kale

   1 tablespoon coconut flakes

   ½ cup coconut milk

   1 tablespoon (1 scoop) BōKU Super Food

How to BōKU
Place all ingredients in a high-powered blender, and blend until smooth, about 30 seconds.

Berry Banana Smoothie

An absolute "classic" smoothie taste you'd find at your favorite smoothie or juice bar, the Berry Banana Smoothie will give the pros a run for their money! Cranberry juice provides tantalizing tartness, which is balanced with the creamy sweetness of almond milk and the smooth consistency of banana. This smoothie will take your taste buds on an unforgettably nutritious and mouthwatering adventure! Add Super Food and Super Berries into the mix for unparalleled whole-food nutrition.

Prep time: 3 minutes   **Serves:** 1

½ cup cranberry juice

½ cup almond milk

1 tablespoon (1 scoop) BōKU Super Food

1 teaspoon (1 scoop) BōKU Super Berries

½ banana

1 cup frozen strawberries

How to BōKU

Put ingredients inside a blender (pour liquids in first to avoid clumping of powders). Blend until smooth and creamy.

Bee Real

We are not surprised there is such a buzz about bee pollen these days; we love this beautiful gift of nature! Bee pollen's tiny little golden beads contain protein and valuable amino acids such as phenylalanine and choline, as well as vitamins (including B vitamin), antioxidants, and minerals. Enjoy these nutritional benefits nestled within a delicious blend of nature's sweet fruit and honey.

Prep time: 5 minutes   **Serves:** 1

- ½ cup almond milk
- 1 tablespoon (1 scoop) BōKU Super Food
- 1 tablespoon coconut oil
- 1 banana
- 1 cup frozen strawberries
- 1 tablespoon raw honey
- 1 tablespoon bee pollen
- Mint leaves for garnish (optional)

How to BōKU

Gather your ingredients together inside a blender (pour liquids in first to avoid clumping of powders). Blend until smooth and garnish with mint if desired.

Orange Cream-sicle Protein Shake

This creamy orange protein shake is a delight to drink and a cinch to make! Tangy yet sweet, it contains enough vegan Super Protein to keep you satisfied until your next meal— not to mention vitamin C from the orange juice and vitamin E from the almond milk!

Prep time: 5 minutes   **Serves:** 1

- ½ cup orange juice (freshly squeezed tastes best!)
- 3 tablespoons (1 scoop) BōKU Super Protein
- ¾ cup vanilla almond milk
- 3–4 ice cubes

How to BōKU

Combine orange juice, vanilla almond milk, and Super Protein in your BōKU Shaker, and shake for 30 seconds or until fully combined. Add in ice cubes and give a few more shakes.

Red, White, and Blueberry Smoothie

Sparklers and fireworks are a must when celebrating America's independence. In this smoothie, the red, white, and blue represent Old Glory's Stars and Stripes. Have a happy Fourth of July, and celebrate throughout the year with this special treat!

Prep time: 10 minutes   **Serves:** 1

- 2½ bananas, divided
- 1 cup almond milk or other non-dairy milk, divided
- 1 tablespoon honey
- ¾ cup frozen strawberries or raspberries
- 3 tablespoons (1 scoop) BōKU Super Protein, divided
- ¾ cup açai juice
- 1 cup frozen or fresh blueberries
- Flaked coconut, BōKU Super Cacao Nibs, and/or strawberries for garnish

How to BōKU

For the white layer, blend 2 bananas, ¾ cup non-dairy milk, honey, and 3 to 4 ice cubes. Pour into a container and store in freezer until needed.

For the red layer, blend the strawberries or raspberries, remaining ½ banana, remaining ¼ cup non-dairy milk, 1½ tablespoons Super Protein, and 3 to 4 ice cubes. Pour into separate container and store in freezer until needed.

For the blue layer, blend together the açai juice, remaining 1½ tablespoons Super Protein, blueberries, and 3 to 4 ice cubes. Pour into separate container and store in freezer until needed.

To serve, divide the red smoothie mix equally among 4 clear glasses (the exact number of servings depends on the size of your smoothies). Next, slowly pour the blue layer on top of your red layer, being sure not to mix the two colors. Lastly, carefully top with the white layer. To garnish, add coconut flakes, Super Cacao Nibs, or strawberries on top!

Red Velvet Smoothie

The **Red Velvet Smoothie,** inspired by red velvet cake batter, not only tastes deliciously dessert-like, but contains antioxidants, anti-inflammatory properties, vitamins, minerals, and energy-boosting superfoods. This delectable blend also offers a dose of potassium, magnesium, iron, dietary fiber, and omega-3 fatty acids.

Prep time: 3 minutes   **Serves:** 1

- 1 tablespoon (1 scoop) BōKU Super Fuel
- 1 tablespoon coconut oil
- 2 dates, pitted
- 1 tablespoon cashews
- 1 cup almond or coconut milk
- 1 banana
- 1 tablespoon BōKU Super Cacao Nibs
- ½ small beet, peeled
- 1 teaspoon chia seeds
- 1–1½ cups ice

How to BōKU

Add all ingredients to a high-powered blender. Blend until smooth and creamy.

Make It All Butter Smoothie

This powerful smoothie features our award-winning energy formula, Super Fuel. Originally designed for elite athletes, Super Fuel is an organic energy powder brimming with super-adaptor phytonutrients; it's perfect for anyone looking for an extra spring in their step. Delight your palate with the flavors of creamy peanut and almond butter, sweet cacao, and balancing coconut.

Prep time: 3 minutes   **Serves:** 1

1 tablespoon (1 scoop) BōKU Super Fuel

2 dates, pitted

2 tablespoons coconut flakes

Pinch sea salt

1 cup almond milk

1 banana

2 tablespoons BōKU Super Cacao Nibs

1½ tablespoons peanut butter

1½ tablespoons almond butter

How to BōKU

Place all ingredients in a high-powered blender. Blend until smooth, about 30 seconds.

Super Peanut Butter Pro

Up, up, and away! Soar to new heights with this smoothie that contains the trifecta of uplifting BōKU Super Food blends: Super Fuel, which is known for its "grounded flight" effect on the body; Super Cacao Nibs (cacao was referred to as the "food of the gods" by ancient cultures); and lastly, Super Protein, which supplies your muscles with the protein they crave. On top of all of that, banana and peanut butter give this powerful concoction a sweet yet balanced taste.

Prep time: 5 minutes   **Serves:** 1

1 cup almond milk (or any non-dairy milk)

1 tablespoon (1 scoop) BōKU Super Fuel

2 tablespoons BōKU Super Cacao Nibs

Optional boost: 1 scoop (1 teaspoon) BōKU Super Shrooms

3 tablespoons (1 scoop) BōKU Super Protein

1 banana

1 tablespoon peanut butter

How to BōKU

Place all ingredients in blender; blend until smooth.

Lost and Found Smoothie

This exotic green smoothie—with bright citrus notes, almond undertones, and the surprising herbaceous pop of basil—is a unique take on the traditional smoothie. BōKU Super Food imparts naturally sourced vitamins, minerals, antioxidants, and pro-biotics that provide super nutrition to help rejuvenate and vitalize. In addition to giving the smoothie a buttery yet light consistency, the spinach provides a multitude of vitamins and minerals, specifically vitamins K and A, manganese, folate, and iron. The orange provides nearly 100 percent of your daily dose of vitamin C.

Prep time: 3 minutes   **Serves:** 1

- 1 tablespoon (1 scoop) BōKU Super Food
- 1 handful spinach
- 1 tablespoon almonds
- 1 orange, peeled
- 5 leaves basil
- 1 banana
- 2 dates, pitted
- ½ cup coconut milk
- ½ cup water

How to BōKU

Place all ingredients in a high-powered blender. Blend until smooth, about 30 seconds.

PB&J Protein Smoothie

Who doesn't love a good old-fashioned PB&J sandwich? We love them so much we created a protein smoothie version so you can chow down (or slurp!) PB&Js in a way your body will appreciate. Just as you can pick a favorite jelly when making a sandwich, you can also tailor this smoothie to your taste buds by changing the berry type.

Prep time: 5 minutes **Serves:** 1

- ¾ cup non-dairy milk (or berry juice of your choice)
- 2 tablespoons peanut butter, or more to taste
- 1–1½ cups frozen or fresh organic berries of your choice
- 1–1½ cups ice
- 3 tablespoons (1 scoop) BōKU Super Protein
- Chia seeds for garnish (optional)

How to BōKU

Blend all ingredients in a high-powered blender until smooth and creamy. Add more peanut butter or berries to taste depending on how you like your PB&J. We like to sprinkle chia seeds on top for extra nutritional value and a delicious crunch!

Peanut Butter Cup Shake

All the taste of a scrumptious peanut butter cup without the guilt! Sip shamelessly on this delectably tempting shake knowing you are taking in more nutrients than most people get in several days with the power of BōKU Super Food!

Prep time: 2 minutes   **Serves:** 1

10 ounces (1¼ cups) vanilla almond milk (or vanilla rice milk if you prefer)

1 tablespoon (1 scoop) BōKU Super Food

2 tablespoons peanut butter

1 tablespoon unsweetened cocoa powder

2–3 ice cubes

How to BōKU

Pour the chocolate hemp milk into your BōKU shaker until it reaches the 10-ounce line. Add in Super Food, peanut butter, cocoa powder, and 2 to 3 ice cubes. Shake until blended.

BōKU Tip

If you'd like your drink sweeter, try adding a drop or two of liquid stevia.

Coco Love Smoothie

This creamy, coconut-based smoothie is a wonderful complement to BōKU Super Protein powder, which gives the smoothie a rich consistency and boasts a serious quantity of highly absorbable, super-nutritious organic protein, along with the full spectrum of amino acids. Coconut flakes are rich in zinc, iron, fiber, and probiotics. Coconut butter is full of amino acids, calcium, and magnesium, and it contains "good" fat (50 percent lauric acid); it is made up mostly of medium-chain fatty acids, which the body metabolizes efficiently and converts into energy, rather than storing as fat. And coconut milk is a quality source of omega-6 fatty acids and is high in iron, magnesium, and potassium.

Prep time: 3 minutes   **Serves:** 1

3 tablespoons (1 scoop) BōKU Super Protein

1 banana

1 tablespoon coconut oil

1 tablespoon coconut butter

2 dates, pitted

2 tablespoons coconut flakes

½ cup coconut milk

½ cup coconut water, plus pulp

Ingredients (lower calorie)

3 tablespoons (1 scoop) BōKU Super Protein

1 banana

2 dates, pitted

½ cup coconut milk

½ cup coconut water, plus pulp

1–1½ cups ice

How to BōKU

Place all ingredients in a high-powered blender. Blend until smooth, about 30 seconds.

Piña Colada Smoothie

You don't need to be on a beach vacation to enjoy the wonderful taste of this tropical classic. This light and refreshing version of a piña colada is a sweet tango of real pineapple and coconut—not to mention that it packs enough protein to tide you over until your next meal.

Prep time: 5 minutes   **Serves:** 1

1 banana

½ cup light coconut milk

2 cups chopped fresh pineapple, plus more for optional garnish

½ cup chilled pineapple juice

3 tablespoons (1 scoop) BōKU Super Protein

1 cup crushed ice

Fresh cherries and BōKU Toasted Coconut Chips for garnish (optional)

How to BōKU

Blend together all ingredients until smooth. Pour in your favorite glass and garnish with fresh pineapple, cherries, and/or Toasted Coconut Chips.

Mango Delight Shake

Besides having Super Food with pure water, this was one of the very first ways we shared BōKU with the world. The mango nectar is naturally very flavorful and is a great medium to blend phytonutrient-dense Super Food with. Even the pickiest of palates won't raise an eyebrow to this delicious nectar blend. Note: Mango nectar is a very sweet beverage. For a lighter taste, try swapping out 3 to 5 ounces of mango nectar with pure water.

Prep time: 2 minutes   **Serves:** 1

1 scoop BōKU Super Food

1¼ cups (10 ounces) mango nectar (or mango juice)

2–3 ice cubes

How to BōKU

Pour mango nectar or juice into your BōKU shaker until it reaches the 10-ounce line. Add in Super Food and ice and shake until fully combined.

Chocolate Lovers Shake

Sweeten up your life with this chocolate and Super Food combo, sure to liven your step while satisfying your sweet tooth! This shake is so delicious, you would never know it is loaded with many functional ingredients from Super Food to help revitalize and rejuvenate. We like to give this one a few extra shakes to increase the frothiness, making the flavors and texture reminiscent of an old-fashioned malt.

Prep time: 2 minutes   **Serves:** 1

1 tablespoon (1 scoop) BōKU Super Food

1¼ cups (10 ounces) chocolate hemp milk
   (may substitute chocolate rice milk or chocolate almond milk if preferred)

2–3 ice cubes

How to BōKU

Pour the chocolate hemp milk into your BōKU shaker until it reaches the 10-ounce line. Add in Super Food and 2 to 3 ice cubes. Shake until ingredients are combined and it looks nice and frothy.

Pumpkin Smoothie

This rich and creamy smoothie—with almost no fat!—has the taste of fall, but can be enjoyed in any season! An enticing favorite, it is full of antioxidants, like alpha- and beta-carotene, which convert into vitamin A in the body. With our plant-based Super Protein and organic phytonutrient Super Food in the mix, it's as easy as pie to create a lively and flourishing body!

Prep time: 5 minutes   **Serves:** 1

¾ cup almond milk

¼ teaspoon cinnamon or pumpkin pie spice

1 tablespoon (1 scoop) BōKU Super Food

1 banana

3 tablespoons (1 scoop) BōKU Triple-Source Vegan Protein

½ cup pumpkin purée

½ cup ice

How to BōKU

Place all ingredients in a high-powered blender. Blend until smooth, about 30 seconds.

BōKU Tip

For variations, try adding ginger for a little spice and metabolic boost or a few dates for a low-glycemic sweetener and fiber.

Parsley-Mango Reset Smoothie

With the hustle and bustle of modern life, it is inevitable that our bodies will be thrown out of balance from time to time. Help yourself regain that balance with this smoothie, which contains superfoods thought to neutralize the toxic buildup. Take control and hit the reset button with this exciting blend of tropical fruits, zesty and flavorful veggies, and revitalizing BōKU Super Food.

Prep time: 5 minutes   **Serves:** 1

1 tablespoon (1 scoop) BōKU Super Food

¼ cup orange juice or water

1 cup frozen mango

1 small handful arugula (or to taste)

1 small handful cilantro (or to taste)

1 handful spinach

1 orange

½ banana

1 small handful parsley

¼ cup water

How to BōKU

Add all ingredients in a high-powered blender. Blend until smooth and creamy.

Berry Happy Smoothie

This antioxidant-filled smoothie doesn't have "happy" in its name by accident. The antioxidants in berries fight oxidative stress caused by free radicals—talk about creating a happy body! All fruits and vegetables contain antioxidants, but nutrient-rich berries are some of the best sources. The added chia seeds are an excellent source of omega-3 fatty acid, fiber, protein, and minerals, including iron, calcium, magnesium, and zinc.

Prep time: 3 minutes   **Serves:** 1

3 tablespoons (1 scoop) BōKU Super Protein

1 banana

1 cup berries of choice

2 dates, pitted

1 teaspoon chia seeds

2 tablespoons almonds

1 cup coconut or almond milk

1–1½ cups ice

Ingredients (lower calorie)

3 tablespoons (1 scoop) BōKU Super Protein

1 banana

1 cup berries of choice

1–1½ cups ice

2 dates, pitted

1 teaspoon chia seeds

1 cup coconut or almond milk

How to BōKU

Place all ingredients in a high-powered blender. Blend until smooth, about 30 seconds.

Carrot Cake Smoothie

The Carrot Cake Smoothie has a flavor profile that mimics the popular cake but is a delicious and highly nutritious alternative. The whole, sprouted brown rice in BōKU Super Protein gives the smoothie a rich consistency and a serious quantity of highly absorbable, super-nutritious organic protein, not to mention the full spectrum of amino acids. Carrot juice provides beta-carotene and vitamins A, B, and E, in addition to many minerals. You won't find all that nutritive power in a baked carrot cake!

Prep time: 3 minutes   **Serves:** 1

- 3 tablespoons (1 scoop) BōKU Super Protein
- 1 banana
- 2 dates, pitted
- ½ teaspoon fresh ginger (optional)

- 1 teaspoon cinnamon
- 2 tablespoons walnuts
- ½ cup almond milk

Ingredients (lower calorie)

- 3 tablespoons (1 scoop) BōKU Super Protein
- 1 banana
- 2 dates, pitted
- 1 teaspoon cinnamon
- 1–1½ cups ice

- 1 tablespoon walnuts
- ½ cup carrot juice
- ½ cup almond milk
- ½ teaspoon fresh ginger (optional)

How to BōKU

Place all ingredients in a high-powered blender. Blend until smooth, about 30 seconds.

Pineapple Apricot Smoothie

This super-fruity smoothie is perfect for anyone just dipping their toes in the superfood world. With the combination of tasty fruit and your favorite fruit juice, you won't even notice you are consuming over 50 functional whole foods found in BōKU Super Food! It's great for picky kids (and adults!) who are hesitant to eat their greens.

Prep time: 3 minutes   **Serves:** 1

¼ cup crushed pineapple

1 fresh apricot, diced

6 strawberries

½ banana

1½ cups water or your favorite juice

3 tablespoons (3 scoops) BōKU Super Food

How to BōKU

Place all ingredients in a high-powered blender (pour liquids in first to avoid clumping of powders). Blend until smooth, about 30 seconds.

Banana Peanut Delight

They say nothing goes better together than peanut butter and jelly, but what about peanut butter and bananas? We think it is a pretty tight competition, and we're sure Elvis would agree! For best results with this delicious smoothie, use an organic, sugar-free peanut butter.

Prep time: 2 minutes   **Serves:** 3

- ½ banana
- 1 cup peanut butter
- 2–3 cups cold soy milk

- 1 tablespoon (1 scoop) BōKU Super Food
- 3 tablespoons honey
- ½ teaspoon ground cinnamon

How to BōKU
Place all ingredients in a high-powered blender. Blend until smooth, about 30 seconds. Serve immediately.

Simple Chocolate Smoothie

You truly cannot go wrong with this chocolatey, simple, and delicious smoothie. This cinch of a recipe is a hit with kids and adults alike, not to mention an easy way to send invigorating phytonutrients straight to your cells in minutes!

Prep time: 3 minutes   **Serves:** 1

- 1 tablespoon (1 scoop) BōKU Super Food
- 1½ cups (12 ounces) chocolate hemp milk
- 1 cup ice (for blender option only)

How to BōKU

Mix together Super Food with hemp milk, using your blender or a shaker bottle to combine thoroughly for a smooth consistency. You can substitute chocolate almond milk or chocolate rice milk if you prefer.

BōKU Tip

For a thicker, blended smoothie, add 1 cup ice and use your blender. For an easy shake on the go, simply add ingredients to your BōKU shaker bottle!

Keep It Green Sunrise Drink

With coconut, mango, and banana as the leading flavors of this smoothie, you may find yourself daydreaming about a tropical vacation. Zesty and vibrant, the Keep It Green Sunrise Drink makes a great breakfast to kick-start your day. Delight in all of the phytonutrients your body craves and the protein that will keep you satisfied until your next meal—thanks to Super Food and Super Protein.

Prep time: 5 minutes   **Serves:** 1

- 1 scoop (1 tablespoon) BōKU Super Food
- 1–2 tablespoons coconut oil
- 1 tablespoon hemp oil

- 1 scoop (3 tablespoons) BōKU Super Protein
- 1 organic banana
- 1 cup organic orange mango juice

How to BōKU

Place all ingredients in a high-powered blender (pour liquids in first to avoid clumping of powders). Blend until smooth, about 30 seconds.

Protein Balanced Smoothie

This smoothie was specifically designed with a balanced protein and carb combo to keep your body kicked into high gear. The perfect solution for those who love blended treats but are watching their calorie intake, this smoothie can easily replace a full meal due to its savvy combination of protein and vitamins (from Super Protein and Super Food!).

Prep time: 3 minutes   **Serves:** 1

1 cup almond milk

3 tablespoons (1 scoop) BōKU Super Protein

1 tablespoon (1 scoop) BōKU Super Food

½ cup frozen mango

½ cup frozen berries

How to BōKU

Place ingredients inside a blender (pour liquids in first to avoid clumping of powders). Press blend, and enjoy!

Mint Condition Smoothie

Give your body the fuel it wants and recovery it needs to be in mint condition for everything from daily life to training for an athletic event. This powerful smoothie contains BōKU Super Fuel, which is filled with high-potency super adaptors (a food or plant that helps the body adapt to stress) and energizing phytonutrients to speed recovery. Triple-Source Vegan Super Protein is readily available for your body to utilize for muscle growth and health.

Prep time: 5 minutes   **Serves:** 1–2

- 1 cup frozen spinach (or 2 cups fresh)
- 1 cup almond milk
- 2 tablespoons (2 scoops) BōKU Super Fuel
- 6 tablespoons (2 scoops) BōKU Triple-Source Vegan Protein
- 3 tablespoons BōKU Super Cacao Nibs
- Small handful fresh mint leaves
- 4 cubes ice or coconut water ice (for added electrolytes and potassium)

How to BōKU

Gather your ingredients together inside a blender (pour liquids in first to avoid clumping of powders). Blend until smooth.

Vanilla Super Shake

This recipe is **super simple** and super delicious. Any kind of non-dairy vanilla milk will work here—choose your favorite! We love to have this in the morning as a quick shake on the go, or even as a midafternoon pick-me-up in place of a snack. Feel great knowing this smooth vanilla drink is packed with essential vitamins and nutrients from Super Food!

Prep time: 2 minutes   **Serves:** 1

  1 tablespoon (1 scoop) BōKU Super Food

  1¼ cups (10 ounces) vanilla almond milk (may substitute vanilla rice milk or vanilla hemp milk if preferred)

  2–3 ice cubes

How to BōKU
Pour the vanilla almond milk into your BōKU shaker until it reaches the 10-ounce line. Add in Super Food and ice cubes. Shake until ingredients are combined and it looks nice and frothy.

Sweet Cinnamon Shake

Everyone loves a **good cinnamon roll!** We are no exception, which is why we created the Sweet Cinnamon Shake, a healthy alternative to the sugary breakfast treat. Start with non-dairy vanilla milk, then add in health-benefitting cinnamon and natural vanilla extract, which contains antioxidants including vanillic acid and vanillin. Top off with a scoop of Super Food for a blast of phytonutrient power, and enjoy this nutritious and drinkable rendition of a cinnamon roll.

Prep: 2 minutes   **Serves:** 1

  1 scoop BōKU uper Food   1 teaspoon cinnamon

  1 teaspoon vanilla extract   2–3 ice cubes

  10 ounces (1¼ cups) vanilla almond milk (or vanilla rice milk if you prefer)

How to BōKU
Pour vanilla almond milk into your BōKU shaker until it reaches the 10-ounce line. Add in Super Food, cinnamon, vanilla, and ice. Shake until fully combined.

Super Sips

Matcha Mint Iced Tea

Matcha Mint Iced Tea is a cool, refreshing beverage that makes a perfect treat any day. This recipe is super quick and easy and tastes delicious! The matcha provides an energy boost that is great for that middle of the day pick-me-up, and the cool mint leaves are a fantastic compliment to the rich green tea flavor.

Prep time: 5 minutes   **Serves:** 2

> **2 cups filtered water**
>
> **2 teaspoons BōKU Super Matcha Green Tea**
>
> **Splash almond milk to taste**
>
> **2 cups crushed ice**
>
> **1 lime, sliced**
>
> **Mint leaves**
>
> **Honey or organic coconut sugar (optional)**

How to BōKU

Using a shaker bottle, shake together the water, Super Matcha Green Tea, and almond milk until there are no clumps. Add the ice, a squeeze of lime, and several mint leaves. Sweeten with honey or coconut sugar if desired. Shake again, pour into glasses, and garnish with slices of lime and some extra mint leaves.

Berry Refreshing Lemonade

Freshly squeezed, tart and sweet, and filled with antioxidants and vitamins, this twist on a classic lemonade recipe is the perfect beverage to quench your guests' thirst and bring a smile to their faces (or maybe a pucker if you like it on the tart side!). This recipe uses fresh strawberries, freshly squeezed lemon juice, and coconut sugar, which contains nutrients that regular table sugar does not have. Fun fact: Coconut sugar contains a form of fiber called inulin that slows the glucose absorption into the bloodstream, which may be why it has a lower glycemic index than regular sugar. Drink up!

Prep time: 5 minutes   **Serves:** 12

> 3 cups strawberries, sliced
>
> 4½ cups freshly squeezed lemon juice
>
> 1½ tablespoons lemon zest
>
> 4 teaspoons (4 scoops) BōKU Super Berries
>
> 9 cups cold water
>
> Coconut sugar to taste

How to BōKU

Place strawberries, lemon juice, lemon zest, and Super Berries in food processor or blender and process until smooth. Strain the purée and pour it into a large serving jug. Add the water and sugar and mix together. (You'll have to play around with the amount of sugar here. Depending on the sweetness of the strawberries and your own preferences, the amount of sugar can vary.) Serve over ice and enjoy!

Bōku Tip

This is a large recipe and will probably have to be made in batches to fit in your food processor or blender.

Matcha Lime Chia Chiller

This cleansing and energy-providing matcha chiller is perfect anytime you need a pick-me-up. Naturally refreshing, coconut water has a nutty taste and is packed with electrolytes, which keep your body properly hydrated so you can be your best you all day long.

Prep time: 10 minutes   **Serves:** 1

- ¾ cup water
- ¾ cup coconut water
- 2 tablespoons chia seeds
- 1 teaspoon BōKU Super Matcha Green Tea
- 1 tablespoon fresh lime juice, or to taste
- Sweetener to taste (1½ teaspoons grade B maple syrup, a few drops liquid stevia, a small pinch stevia powder, or the sweetener of your choice)

How to BōKU

Add the water, coconut water, chia seeds, and Super Matcha Green Tea to a glass (or BōKU shaker) and mix well. Let sit for 10 minutes to allow the chia seeds to absorb liquid. Add the lime juice and sweetener to taste. Shake or stir to combine and enjoy!

Super Cacao Tea

Warm, soothing, and delicious, this tea is reminiscent of a steaming cup of hot chocolate (without all the sugar and toxic chemicals)! If you are a coffee person, we invite you to try swapping out your morning cup of joe for this antioxidant-filled super drink. Super Cacao Nibs are naturally caffeine free; however, they do contain theobromine, a slightly milder and longer-lasting alternative said to increase your feeling of well-being. If you wish, spice things up by using cinnamon, cloves, or nutmeg!

Prep time: 1 minute   **Cook time:** 2–5 minutes   **Serves:** 1

  1 tablespoon BōKU Super Cacao Nibs

  1 cup hot water

  Creamer of choice (we like to use organic coconut creamer)

How to BōKU

Place water and Super Cacao Nibs in a pot on the stovetop. Turn heat to medium and steep for 2 to 5 minutes, softening the cacao nibs and allowing their flavor to release. Carefully pour contents into your favorite mug and add a splash of creamer.

Spicy BōKU Mary

Tangy and spicy, this nonalcoholic Bloody Mary is a delicious and fun way to drink your veggies! Play around with the ingredients in this classic "mocktail" to suit your taste buds. Like it hot? Turn up the heat by adding more Tabasco!

Prep time: 5 minutes   **Serves:** 1

- 1 tablespoon (1 scoop) BōKU Super Food
- 1 cup tomato juice
- 2 pinches salt and pepper
- 2 dashes Tabasco sauce (or more to taste)
- 2 pinches celery salt
- 1 tablespoon dill pickle juice
- 3–5 ice cubes
- 1 dill pickle spear for garnish (optional)
- 1 celery stalk for garnish (optional)
- 1 slice lime for garnish (optional)
- Green olives for garnish (optional)

How to BōKU

Put all ingredients in your BōKU shaker and shake until combined. If desired, remove lid and add garnishes of pickle, celery, lime, and green olives.

Hot Matcha Latte

First consumed during China's Tang dynasty and later brought to Japan by priests and monks, matcha green tea has a famous legacy that has been befittingly earned. This hot latte is a modern spin on its royal beginning, when the tea was simply mixed with hot water and sipped out of a handcrafted bowl.

Prep time: 5 minutes   **Cook time:** 5 minutes   **Serves:** 1

- ¼ cup boiling water
- 1 teaspoon BōKU Super Matcha Green Tea
- 2 teaspoons organic maple syrup or honey
- 1 cup unsweetened almond milk, steamed or heated

How to BōKU

Combine boiling water, Super Matcha Green Tea, and maple syrup in your favorite coffee cup and mix well. Heat the almond milk over the stovetop or use a milk frother. Pour the hot milk into the mug with the matcha mixture and enjoy!

BōKU Tip

If you feel like getting fancy, we invite you to try some beginner's latte foam art. To make the design pictured, simply space out small dollops of frothed milk on top of your matcha mixture. Take the end of a skewer or tip of a thin knife and drag through the dollops, connecting them all on the same line.

Super Berries Tea

This simple and healing tea uses nature's best to help soothe, restore, and detoxify your system from the inside out—not to mention that it tastes amazing! Super Berries brings a burst of antioxidants, while the lemon and ginger use their natural purifying properties to help you feel your best.

Prep time: 1 minute   **Cook time:** 2–5 minutes   **Serves:** 1

- 1 cup hot water
- 2 teaspoons (2 scoops) BōKU Super Berries (plus more if desired)
- 2 or 3 thin slices lemon
- 1 slice ginger (optional)

How to BōKU

Place water, Super Berries, lemon, and ginger (if using) in a pot on the stovetop. Turn heat to medium and steep for 2 to 5 minutes, allowing all flavors to release. Carefully pour contents into your favorite mug. Let cool slightly and enjoy!

Snacks, Dips & Dressings

Sweet and Spicy Almonds

Give your palette the best of both worlds with a pinch of sweet and a dash of spicy mixed in with your almonds. The added Super Food takes this savory recipe to the next level with over 50 functional super-powered whole foods. Feel free to "go nuts" and add in a mix of cashews, walnuts, pecans, and other nuts if desired!

Prep time: Up to 3 days   **Serves:** 3

1 cup dehydrated raw almonds

1 tablespoon sea salt, plus more to taste

1 tablespoon maple syrup

1 tablespoon (1 scoop) BōKU Super Food

1 tablespoon agave nectar

Seeds from ½ vanilla bean, scraped

¼ teaspoon cayenne (or to taste)

How to BōKU

To prepare the almonds, you will need to soak and dehydrate them, which takes between 24 hours and 3 days. The time difference depends on how long you want to soak the nuts and how dry you prefer them when dehydrating. The longer they soak, the more nutrient-dense they become.

Start the sprouting process by placing the almonds in a resealable container and cover with 1 inch filtered water. Stir in the sea salt and cover. Soak at least 6 hours (and up to 3 days) to activate the dormant nutrients in the raw nuts. Drain the water every day and refill with additional filtered water, but do not add salt again. Store in the refrigerator until ready to use.

To dehydrate the almonds, preheat oven to 150°F. Drain and pat the almonds dry. Then, place them on a parchment paper–covered baking tray, spreading the nuts evenly. Bake for 12 to 24 hours, turning occasionally until they have reached the level of dryness you desire. The almonds are now ready to be used in the recipe or stored for later use.

In a medium bowl, stir together the maple syrup, agave nectar, vanilla seeds, cayenne, and Super Food with a silicone spatula. Add in the almonds and stir until evenly coated.

Line a baking sheet with wax paper. Spread the nuts evenly on the baking sheet and sprinkle with sea salt to taste. Eat right away or store in resealable container for up to a month.

BōKU Tip

To speed up the sprouting and dehydrating process you can purchase pre-sprouted dehydrated nuts. It is important to soak the almonds not only to activate dormant nutrients but also to neutralize the enzyme inhibitors found in them.

Caliente Cauli Bites with Super Buffalo Shroom Sauce

Cauliflower is a very versatile veggie and a unique superfood! Often underused, it's great for a variety of favorites—including cauliflower pizza crust, mashed cauliflower, and of course this recipe! Everyone will love the Cauli Bites' hot wing–like flavor and the benefits of the spicy and immune-boosting Super Shroom sauce.

Prep time: 15 minutes   **Cook time:** 20 minutes   **Serves:** about 6

Cauli Bites

1 large head (about 3 pounds) cauliflower, stemmed and leaves removed

¼ cup extra-virgin olive oil

1 teaspoon sea salt

1 tablespoon cumin powder

1 teaspoon whole fennel seed, ground

1 tablespoon Thai or red chili flake powder

1 tablespoon whole Sichuan peppercorns, ground and seeds removed

1 tablespoon brown sugar

¼ cup fine bread crumbs

Sauce

2 tablespoons vegan butter

1 cup buffalo hot sauce

1 teaspoon (1 scoop) BōKU Super Shrooms

How to BōKU

and grease a baking sheet with oil.

Place the cauliflower in a large saucepan filled with ¾ inch water and cover. Cook on medium heat for 8 to 10 minutes or until the cauliflower is tender yet still crisp. Drain and set aside.

Meanwhile, place the olive oil in a large mixing bowl. When cauliflower is cool enough to handle, start cutting the florets off the head in large pieces; then, slice them in half to make bite-size pieces. (This makes a flat side and larger surface area to coat and brown while cooking.) Toss the cauliflower bites in the oil and set aside.

To make the coating, in a small pan on low heat, add the salt, cumin, ground fennel, ground chili powder, and ground Sichuan peppercorns. Toast spices, stirring continuously, until they become aromatic, about 3 to 5 minutes. Transfer half the spice mixture to the mixing bowl. Toss lightly with the cauliflower. Taste, and add more of the spice mixture if you like. Then, add the sugar and bread crumbs and toss until all the bites are evenly coated.

Place the coated cauliflower on the baking sheet, making sure the pieces have space between them. Roast on the middle rack for 15 minutes; then, stir and return them to the oven for another 5 minutes or until you see that the face-down edges are toasted.

Meanwhile, to make the sauce, melt the vegan butter in a saucepan and stir in the hot sauce until both are combined. Pour into a serving dish for dipping and stir in the Super Shrooms. Serve with the roasted Caliente Cauli Bites.

Super Tapenade

Warning: This tapenade is addictively delicious! This zesty dip, spread, or sandwich filling comes together quickly with a few prepared products you already have in the pantry. We love to put this on top of sliced and toasted baguette rounds for a nutrition-packed appetizer, snack, or side dish.

Prep time: 5 minutes   **Serves:** 5

1 (7-ounce) jar roasted red peppers, drained

1 (6-ounce) jar marinated artichoke hearts, drained

½ cup pitted Kalamata olives

2 tablespoons (2 scoops) BōKU Super Food

1 small shallot, minced

¼ cup loosely packed fresh basil leaves, chopped

2 tablespoons extra-virgin olive oil

2 teaspoons red wine vinegar

Sea salt and pepper to taste

French baguette, oil of choice to lightly coat toasted bread (optional)

How to BōKU

Place the roasted red peppers, artichoke hearts, and olives in the bowl of a food processor fitted with a metal blade. Process to small pieces; then pulse in the Super Food and turn mixture out into a bowl. Add the shallot, basil, oil, and vinegar, and stir to combine well. Add sea salt and black pepper to taste.

BōKU Tip

Grab your favorite crackers, chips, or toasted bread slices from the store and spoon desired amount of tapenade on each one (usually enough to cover most of the top). If you would like to make your own toasted bread slices, take a French baguette and slice desired number of ½-inch rounds. Preheat oven to 300°F. Cover a baking sheet with foil and lightly coat with oil. Place the bread slices close together on the sheet and lightly coat them with oil as well. Sprinkle with pepper and sea salt. Bake for 15 to 20 minutes, or until golden brown. Allow to cool on a cookie rack or plate. Once cool, top slices with tapenade or place in an airtight container to store at room temperature for up to one week.

Antioxidant Strawberry Salsa

We love the good-ole tomato/onion/cilantro salsa combo as much as the next person. But in celebration of the taste of summer, we created a blend of strawberries and balsamic vinegar with Super Berries for an extra antioxidant boost! Let's not forget all the vitamin C you'll naturally be soaking up from the delicious strawberry base. Added bonus: No shame for hanging around the dip bowl—this recipe is absolutely guiltless!

Prep time: 5 minutes   **Serves:** 6–8

2 tablespoons lemon juice

1 tablespoon extra-virgin olive oil

1½ tablespoons honey

2 tablespoons balsamic vinegar

¼ teaspoon salt

Pinch ground pepper

½ shallot, minced

1 pound strawberries, diced

6 basil leaves, thinly sliced

2 teaspoons (2 scoops) BōKU Super Berries

How to BōKU

Combine all ingredients in a large mixing bowl. You can eat the salsa immediately or chill it in the refrigerator for use later that day. Enjoy with pita chips (cinnamon or plain), tortilla chips, or even as a topping on a side dish or dessert.

Lettuce Wraps
with Peanut Dipping Sauce

This super-fresh dish is an easy rendition of the exotic spring rolls and delicious peanut sauce you typically would only find when dining out; however, now you have the luxury of making them at home in minutes. Plus, they're even fresher and better with the power of Super Shrooms.

Prep time: 15 minutes   **Makes:** 6 wraps

Peanut sauce

¼ cup creamy peanut butter

1 tablespoon hoisin sauce

2 teaspoons soy sauce

1 clove garlic, mashed (about 1 teaspoon minced)

1 teaspoon Sriracha sauce or a chile garlic sauce (optional, for spice)

1 teaspoon (1 scoop) BōKU Super Shrooms

1–2 tablespoons warm water, or more as needed

Handful fresh cilantro (optional)

Wraps

1 head butter lettuce, leaves separated

1 yellow bell pepper, julienned

1 red bell pepper, julienned

1 large carrot, peeled and sliced

⅓ cup chopped red cabbage ¼

1 avocado, sliced (optional)

How to BōKU

To make the peanut sauce, whisk all sauce ingredients except water together in a bowl or blend in a food processor. Add the water, a little at a time, until you reach the desired consistency. Pour into a serving bowl and top with cilantro if desired. Set aside.

To assemble the wraps, place your desired amount of precut veggies and optional avocado in the middle of each butter lettuce leaf. Drizzle with peanut sauce before wrapping, or wrap first and use the peanut sauce as a dipping sauce.

Kale-Yeah Chips!

Who could have thought that leafy greens and nutritional yeast could make such a crunchy and addictive chip? Super Shrooms add a deepened flavor as well as an immunity boost to these delicious crisps. Say good-bye to regular greasy chips and hello to your new favorite snack!

Prep time: 10 minutes   **Cook time:** 50 minutes   **Serves:** 5–6

   1 bunch kale

   2 tablespoons extra-virgin olive oil

   ½ cup nutritional yeast

   1 teaspoon (1 scoop) BōKU Super Shrooms

   ½ teaspoon salt

How to BōKU

Preheat oven to 300°F. Line a large baking sheet with parchment paper or foil.

Wash and dry kale very thoroughly. Remove leaves from thick stems and tear into large "chip" pieces (they will shrink!). Add kale chips to a large bowl and massage oil into leaves, being sure to get the ridges.

In a separate bowl, combine the nutritional yeast, Super Shrooms, and salt. Sprinkle mixture onto kale leaves in your large bowl and toss to coat evenly.

Spread half the kale pieces on the baking sheet and bake for about 25 minutes, rotating the baking sheet every 5 to 7 minutes to ensure the chips bake evenly. Repeat with second batch.

Vegan Super Shroom Gravy

Rich in essential vitamins and minerals, this hearty gravy features BōKU's Super Shrooms, which blend perfectly with sautéed cremini mushrooms and a few other simple, savory ingredients. Pour it over cauliflower mashed potatoes (try our Cauliflower Shroom Mash-Up on page 87), seared tempeh, or your favorite protein.

Prep time: 5 minutes   **Cook time:** 25 minutes   **Serves:** 4

4 tablespoons vegetable oil, divided

4 ounces cremini mushrooms, stems trimmed and sliced ¼-inch thick

Salt and freshly ground black pepper

1 medium shallot, diced

2 bay leaves

¼ cup red wine

⅓ cup all-purpose flour

4 teaspoons (4 scoops) BōKU Super Shrooms

1 teaspoon soy sauce

2 cups mushroom broth

How to BōKU

Heat 1 tablespoon oil in a large pan over medium-high heat until shimmering. Add mushrooms, season with salt and pepper, and cook until softened, about 3 minutes. Transfer mushrooms to a heatproof bowl and set aside. Add remaining 3 tablespoons oil to the pan and heat on medium until shimmering. Add shallot, bay leaves, and salt and pepper to taste, and sauté for 3 minutes, or until shallots are softened. Mix in wine and cook until wine has almost completely evaporated.

In a separate large pan on medium heat, whisk flour, Super Shrooms, soy sauce, and broth until gravy has thickened, about 3 minutes. Stir reserved mushrooms and reduced wine mixture into the gravy. Season with additional salt and pepper as needed. Remove bay leaves before serving.

Super Berries Vinaigrette Dressing

Your favorite refreshing drink powder has added a new talent to its repertoire. We now present to you—drum roll, please—Super Berries Vinaigrette Dressing! All of the things you love about Super Berries can now be enjoyed atop your favorite salad: the berry blitz of anti-oxidants, the freeze-dried "locked in" nutrition, and the delectable and fresh berry taste are all right there ready to amaze your taste buds and satiate your tummy. Not to mention that Super Berries uses the darkest pigmented berries from around the world, so remember, "the darker the berry, the more extraordinary!"

Prep time: 5 minutes   **Makes:** about ½ cup (simply double recipe for a larger crowd!)

   1½ teaspoons Dijon mustard

   2 tablespoons fresh orange juice

   2 tablespoons extra-virgin olive oil

   1 tablespoon honey

   1–1½ tablespoons rice vinegar (to taste)

   2 teaspoons (2 scoops) BōKU Super Berries

How to BōKU

Combine mustard, orange juice, olive oil, honey, and vinegar in small bowl or BōKU shaker. Whisk or shake until thoroughly combined. Next, add Super Berries and whisk or shake until smooth. Drizzle over your favorite salad!

BōKU Tip

We like to enjoy this dressing over a simple salad of baby spinach leaves, slivered almonds, chia seeds, and sliced strawberries. Assorted berries and sliced avocado can also be added for extra flavor and nutritional content!

Black Bean Dip

Nothing says snack or party time like bean dip, but who knew it could be so nutrition-packed? Black beans are known for their fiber, potassium, folate, vitamin B6, and phytonutrient content. Combine this with cleansing cilantro, thermogenesis-increasing chili powder (meaning your body produces heat, therefore burning more calories), and phytonutrient-loaded Super Food for a dip that your body and your taste buds will love!

Prep time: 10 minutes   **Serves:** 4

1 (15-ounce) can black beans, drained and rinsed

2 tablespoons white onion, chopped

2 tablespoons chopped cilantro

1 clove garlic, chopped

½ teaspoon cumin

½ teaspoon red chili powder

Pinch Mexican oregano

1 tablespoon (1 scoop) BōKU Super Food

2 limes, juiced

2–3 dashes your favorite hot sauce (or to taste)

Sea salt (to taste)

How to BōKU

Place all ingredients in the bowl of a food processor and blend to a smooth consistency. If desired, warm on stovetop or in oven.

BōKU Tip

Grab a bag of your favorite chips from the store to enjoy with your dip (we love organic blue corn chips!). For a more filling appetizer, thinly slice a baguette and serve alongside the dip.

BōKU Avocado-Lime Dip

This avocado-lime dip with Super Food boost is a perfect companion to a bowl of baked chips, a platter of pita bread, or a couple of crackers. The smooth avocado, spicy salsa, jalapeño pepper, and zesty lime make this a fantastic snack for all occasions.

Prep: 5 minutes　　**Serves:** 4

　　2 large ripe avocados

　　½ cup diced jalapeño or serrano pepper

　　¼ cup prepared green salsa

　　¼ cup chopped cilantro

　　¼ cup chopped red onion

　　1 teaspoon lime zest

　　1 tablespoon (1 scoop) BōKU Super Food

　　1 plump scallion, roughly chopped

　　½ lime, juiced

　　Sea salt to taste

How to BōKU

Place all ingredients in medium-sized bowl. Use a fork to mash avocado and mix all ingredients together.

Soups, Salads & Sides

White Bean and Super Shrooms Soup

At the end of the day, there is nothing more comforting and cozy then settling down with a steaming bowl of savory and delicious soup. This soup makes a stop at all the nutritive bases. It boasts white beans, which have fiber and protein (plus, they're seriously delicious), as well as kale, which is rich in vitamins and minerals. What makes this recipe a true home run is the BōKU Super Shrooms, a functional, protective powerhouse for your overall well-being that also adds an amazing depth to the taste of this super soup.

Prep time: 30–120 minutes, depending on bean size   **Cook time:** 40 minutes   **Serves:** 6–8

1 pound dried white beans (such as cannellini, navy, or Great Northern), rinsed

¼ cup extra-virgin olive oil

1 large carrot, peeled and chopped

2 celery stalks, chopped

1 large yellow onion, chopped

5 cloves garlic, minced

5 teaspoons (5 scoops) BōKU Super Shrooms

Salt and pepper

6 cups vegetable stock

1 (14.5-ounce) can diced tomatoes

3 fresh thyme sprigs

1 bay leaf

1½ pounds kale

¼ cup roughly chopped basil leaves

Grated vegan cheese for garnish (optional—we like almond cheese!)

How to BōKU

Put the beans in a large pot and add enough water to cover by 2 to 3 inches. Cover and bring to a boil; then lower the heat to a simmer. Cook, stirring occasionally, until the beans are tender, between 30 minutes to 2 hours, depending on the size of the beans. Season with salt. (You can do this step a day or two ahead of time if you choose. Just cool the beans, transfer them to an airtight container with their cooking liquid, and refrigerate until you are ready to make the soup.)

To make the soup, pour the olive oil into a large pot over medium-high heat. When it's nice and hot, add the carrot, celery, onion, garlic, and Super Shrooms. Season with salt and pepper. Cook, stirring frequently, until the vegetables are very soft, about 12 to 15 minutes. Add the drained beans along with the stock, tomatoes, thyme, and bay leaf. Stir, bring to a boil, and cover. Then, lower the heat so the soup simmers steadily. Cook for 15 minutes.

Meanwhile, remove the thick stems and ribs from the kale and discard. Roughly chop the leaves. Stir the kale into the soup, cover, and cook until the kale is tender, about 10 minutes. Remove the thyme sprigs and bay leaf. Stir in the basil and adjust the seasoning. Serve hot, garnished with grated cheese, if desired. Store leftover soup in an airtight container in the refrigerator for up to several days.

Quick Chilled Lima Bean Soup

No pot, no pan, no problem! All you need to make this easy soup is a high-speed blender and a few key ingredients. The lima-bean base offers many functional nutritional components such as insoluble fiber, folate, magnesium, and iron. To complement the beans, we use vitamin-rich tomato juice and stimulating curry. Perfect for a warm summer evening, this is a favorite in our California-based BōKU office.

Prep time: 5 minutes   **Serves:** 4

   2½ cups tomato juice

   2 cups plain almond or soy yogurt

   1 (10-ounce) package frozen lima beans

   1 teaspoon curry powder

   ¼ cup (4 scoops) BōKU Super Food

   Salt and pepper to taste

How to BōKU

In a high-powered blender, place the tomato juice, yogurt, frozen lima beans, curry powder, and BōKU. Blend until smooth and add salt and pepper to taste.

Super Shrooms Miso Soup

Functional mushrooms have been utilized for centuries by the Chinese, Egyptians, and Romans for their wonderful nutritional value. They were also associated with well-being and longevity, and were even included in the diet of the royal family. Treat yourself and your family like royalty with this quick and easy mushroom miso soup featuring Super Shrooms. It is low in fat and high in protective properties; plus, it boasts antioxidants! For a heartier soup, try stirring in cubes of your favorite tofu, which will add protein to this already health-enhancing and gratifying dish.

Prep time: 5 minutes   **Cook time:** 5–10 minutes   **Serves:** 4

- 4 cups water
- 3–4 tablespoons white or red miso (to taste)
- 4 teaspoons (4 scoops) BōKU Super Shrooms
- ½ cup organic red quinoa, cooked
- 6 medium shiitake mushrooms, sliced
- Chopped green onion, to taste
- 1 cup cubed tofu (optional)

How to BōKU

Heat water in a medium saucepan. Add miso to taste. When miso broth starts to simmer, add Super Shrooms, cooked quinoa, mushrooms, and green onion to taste. If desired, add cubed tofu for a heartier soup, making sure to let the tofu get nice and hot in the broth before serving.

Fresh Fruit Salad

One of our favorite ways to start the day or to put together a quick, healthy snack is by mixing a colorful array of fresh fruit together with BōKU Super Berries, which are gathered from the most pristine, exotic, organic sources around the world and dried slowly to lock in their phytonutrients.

Prep time: 5–10 minutes **Makes:** 2+ cups

- Honeydew melon, cubed
- Cantaloupe, cubed
- Pineapple, cubed
- Kiwi, cut into rounds or half-moon slices
- Blueberries
- Banana, sliced
- Strawberries, sliced
- Raspberries
- Grapes
- 1 tablespoon (3 scoops) BōKU Super Berries for every 2 cups fruit
- 1 orange, juiced

How to BōKU

This recipe is very versatile and quick to make if you purchase pre-sliced fruit such as melon and pineapple. If you slice all your own fruit and want to have this delicious healthy snack or breakfast on multiple days, store the extra sliced fruit and juice together in the refrigerator for up to 3 days. You can prepare as much or as little fruit salad as you like—just add 1 tablespoon Super Berries for every 2 cups fruit. Mix together your favorite fruits or the ones listed above, and stir in the Super Berries just before the orange juice.

Super Sprout Salad

This superfood-packed salad hits all the right contrasting notes with the buttery crunch of brussels sprouts, the earthy sweet flavor of kale, and the zesty kick of lemon and Dijon mustard, balanced out by a few other flavorful ingredients and BōKU Super Food.

Prep time: 15–20 minutes   **Serves:** 6

  1½ bunches kale, stemmed and thinly sliced

  2 lemons, juiced

  1½ tablespoons Dijon mustard

  ½ shallot, minced

  1 clove garlic, minced

  2 pinches sea salt

  ground black pepper, to taste

  1 tablespoon (1 scoop) BōKU Super Food

  ½ cup extra-virgin olive oil

  12 brussels sprouts, ends trimmed and thinly sliced

  ⅓ cup raw sliced almonds for garnish

How to BōKU

Place the sliced kale in a large bowl, making sure that the leaves are very dry. In a small bowl or measuring cup, stir together the lemon juice, mustard, shallot, garlic, salt, pepper, and Super Food. Then, whisk in the oil until it is completely combined. Add three quarters of the dressing to the kale, and massage it into the leaves with your hands. Toss the sliced brussels sprouts with the marinated kale until well combined. Plate your desired amount of salad and top each portion with a tablespoon sliced almonds.

Vegan Wild Rice Stuffing

This stuffing made of wild rice, shallots, BōKU Super Golden Berries, and mushrooms is wildly delicious! Naturally gluten free, vegan, protein rich, and high in fiber, this recipe is a winner all the way around and makes a perfect addition to any meal. You don't have to be a vegan to appreciate the great taste of this wild rice stuffing.

Prep time: 15 minutes   **Cook time:** 35–45 minutes   **Serves:** 12–15

- 2 quarts vegetable stock
- 3 cups wild rice, rinsed
- 1 pinch sea salt
- 1 tablespoon olive oil
- 6 large shallots, chopped
- 6 cloves garlic, minced
- 1 pound white mushrooms, thinly sliced
- Freshly ground black pepper
- 1 tablespoon soy sauce or wheat-free tamari
- 1 teaspoon dried thyme
- ½ cup BōKU Super Golden Berries
- 1 cup chopped fresh parsley
- ⅓ cup chopped fresh sage

How to BōKU

In a large saucepan, bring the stock to a boil. Add the rice and salt and return to a boil. Reduce the heat, cover, and simmer for 35 to 45 minutes, or until the water is absorbed. Remove from heat. Heat the olive oil in a large pan, add the shallots and garlic, and cook for about 10 minutes, or until golden. Add the mushrooms and continue to cook, stirring occasionally, until the mushrooms release their juices; then, stir in the pepper, soy sauce, and thyme. Cook until the liquid evaporates. Transfer mushroom mixture to a large bowl along with the rice. Add the Super Golden Berries, parsley, and sage and toss to combine. Taste and adjust the seasonings, adding more pepper if necessary. Store in the refrigerator up to 3 days.

Super Quinoa Salad

An ancient grain, quinoa is naturally gluten free and one of the few plant foods that is considered a complete protein, which makes this recipe a well-balanced salad for lunch, snack, or dinner.

Prep time: 10 minutes   **Cook time:** 10 minutes   **Serves:** 4–6

½ cup quinoa

4 tablespoons feta (omit for vegan version)

½ cucumber, sliced thickly

¼ cup fresh basil, chopped

2 green onions, green and white parts chopped

2 cups cherry tomatoes, sliced

1 garlic clove, minced

1 tablespoon (1 scoop) BōKU Super Food

2 tablespoons olive oil

1 lemon, juiced

Salt and pepper to taste

Chopped fresh parsley for garnish (optional)

How to BōKU

Cook the quinoa according to the package directions. Set aside to cool.

In a large bowl mix together the feta, cucumber, basil, green onions, cherry tomatoes, garlic, and Super Food. Mix in the olive oil, lemon juice, and cooled quinoa; toss to combine. Add salt and pepper to taste. Let the salad sit for a few minutes to let the flavors meld; taste again and add more salt if needed. Garnish with parsley if desired. Serve immediately or cover and refrigerate.

Cauliflower Shroom Mash-Up

People we've made this super-simple side for are pleasantly surprised at its deliciousness. A healthy substitute for mashed potatoes, this cauliflower mash contains B vitamins, carotenoids, and phytonutrients. It also boasts the longevity-promoting benefits of BōKU Super Shrooms. Try this out with our Vegan Super Shroom Gravy (page 67) on top for a double dose of Super Shrooms power!

Prep time: 5 minutes　　**Cook time:** 10 minutes　　**Makes:** about 6 cups

- 1 medium head cauliflower, stemmed and cut into florets
- 2–3 medium cloves garlic, finely chopped
- 1 tablespoon extra-virgin olive oil or vegan butter
- 6 teaspoons (6 scoops) BōKU Super Shrooms
- Sea salt and ground black pepper to taste

How to BōKU

Bring a large pot of salted water to the boil. Add the cauliflower and cook for about 10 minutes or until very tender. Drain, reserving ¼ cup cooking liquid. Place the cooked cauliflower into a food processor fitted with an S-blade. Add the garlic, oil, and reserved water, 1 tablespoon at a time, along with the Super Shrooms. Purée until smooth (or mash cauliflower with a potato masher). Season with salt and pepper and serve.

Gingered Wild Rice and Roasted Squash Salad

This savory dish is a trinity of smooth, earthy, and full-bodied flavors. An exciting trip for your taste buds, the blend of vegetables over wild rice tossed in a ginger dressing will have the whole table saying wow! As a nod to its unique chestnut-like flavor, the red kuri squash is known as *potimarron* in France, a combination of the French words pumpkin (*potiron*) and chestnut (*marron*).

Prep time: 10 minutes   **Cook time:** 15 minutes   **Serves:** 5

- 1 red kuri squash (or other orange-fleshed winter squash), peeled and cut into 1-inch cubes
- 1 red onion, thinly sliced
- Sea salt to taste
- 1½ tablespoons apple cider vinegar
- 1 tablespoon apple juice
- 1 tablespoon (1 scoop) BōKU Super Food

- 2 teaspoons grated fresh ginger
- ½ teaspoon five-spice powder
- 2 teaspoons honey
- 3 tablespoons olive oil, plus more for drizzling
- 8 ounces wild rice, prepared according to package directions and cooled
- 1 cup cashews

How To BōKU

Preheat oven to 400°F. Toss the squash and onions together in a bowl with a light drizzle of olive oil and a sprinkle of sea salt. Turn onto baking sheet and roast 30 minutes or until tender, stirring halfway through. Remove from oven and allow to cool while you prepare the dressing.

To make the dressing, in a small bowl whisk together the vinegar, apple juice, Super Food, ginger, five-spice powder, and honey. Let rest a few minutes. Whisk in olive oil, and add salt to taste. Toss the rice and squash mixture with the ginger dressing. Check for seasoning. Fold in the cashews.

Bōku Breakfasts

Raw Quinoa Breakfast Blend

This gluten-free super breakfast is as delicious as it is healthy! Whip up this raw and sweet concoction to jump-start your day with just the right amount of protein, fiber, and antioxidants. Complete with BōKU Super Maca and Super Cacao Nibs, it is sure to give you a boost of energy, put some spring in your step, and start your day strong.

Prep time: 5–10 minutes   **Serves:** 2

1 tablespoon quinoa flakes

2 tablespoons gluten-free oats

1 tablespoon chia seeds

1 tablespoon raw cacao powder

1 teaspoon BōKU Super Maca

3 cups coconut water, divided

2 ripe bananas

1 tablespoon BōKU Super Cacao Nibs for garnish

Nuts of choice, dried mulberries, and goji berries for garnish (optional)

How to BōKU

Mix together quinoa flakes, oats, chia seeds, cacao powder, and Super Maca. Stir in 1 cup coconut water and set aside. Meanwhile, blend bananas and remaining 2 cups coconut water in blender. Pour banana mixture over cereal and enjoy! Garnish with Super Cacao Nibs, optional nuts, mulberries, and goji berries.

Berry Delicious Pancakes

Hotcakes, flapjacks, johnnycakes . . . no matter the name, we *love* these fluffy breakfast favorites! Try out this spin on a classic pancake recipe with fresh blueberries along with vitamin- and mineral-filled BōKU Super Berries. Fresh, fruity, and brimming with antioxidants, these are sure to be a hit at the breakfast table.

Prep: 10 minutes   **Cook:** 10 minutes   **Makes:** 6 pancakes

1 cup flour (we like to use organic whole wheat flour)

3–5 tablespoons BōKU Super Berries (to taste)

1 tablespoon baking powder

¼ teaspoon salt

1 cup almond milk or non-dairy milk of choice

2 tablespoons olive oil or melted coconut oil

2 tablespoons maple syrup or sugar of choice

1 teaspoon pure vanilla extract

½ cup fresh blueberries

Additional oil or butter to grease your pan/skillet if necessary

How to BōKU

In a medium bowl, whisk together the flour, Super Berries, baking powder, and salt. In a separate bowl mix together the milk, oil, maple syrup, and vanilla extract. Next, pour your liquid mixture into the dry mixture and combine until only a few lumps remain. Then carefully fold in blueberries. Let sit for 5 minutes.

If necessary, lightly spray pan or electric skillet (preheated to 350°F), with cooking oil.

Scoop ¼ cup batter onto the hot skillet and cook for about 2 to 3 minutes or until small bubbles form. Flip and cook the opposite side until light golden brown. Repeat this process with the remaining batter, adjusting heat if necessary. Enjoy with organic maple syrup, fresh berries, and even more Super Berries sprinkled on top if desired.

Matcha Chia Pudding

Cha-cha-cha-chia! Try this energizing breakfast packed with fiber, omega-3s, antioxidants, and anti-inflammatory compounds. Easy to make, raw, and vegan, this breaky contains as much caffeine as a cup of coffee. This is the ultimate breakfast of chia champions!

Prep time: 5 minutes   **Serves:** 1

>   **4 tablespoons chia seeds, divided**
>
>   **1 cup almond milk (or other non-dairy milk)**
>
>   **1 tablespoon rolled oats**
>
>   **1–2 tablespoons organic maple syrup, plus more for serving if desired**
>
>   **1 teaspoon vanilla**
>
>   **½ teaspoon BōKU Super Matcha Green Tea**
>
>   **Fresh fruit for serving (optional)**

How to BōKU

Blend 1 tablespoon chia seeds in a blender with almond milk, oats, maple syrup, vanilla, and Super Matcha Green Tea. Pour mixture into a bowl and stir in remaining 3 tablespoons chia seeds.

Cover and refrigerate at least 3 hours (or overnight!) until your pudding is the perfect consistency. Enjoy with maple syrup or fresh fruit on top (or both!).

Super Cacao Cakes

Step outside the box mix and try making these delicious and fluffy pancakes from scratch! These vegan pancakes are comprised of "better for you" ingredients such as whole wheat flour, almond milk, and coconut oil. Instead of using chocolate chips, we traded up for Super Cacao Nibs, the least processed and most natural form of chocolate. These little nibs have antioxidants, flavonoids, magnesium, and potassium!

Prep time: 10 minutes   **Cook time:** 10 minutes   **Makes:** 6 pancakes

- **1 cup flour (we like to use organic whole wheat flour)**
- **1 tablespoon baking powder**
- **¼ teaspoon salt**
- **1 cup almond milk or non-dairy milk of choice**
- **2 tablespoons olive oil or melted coconut oil, plus more to grease pan if necessary**
- **2 tablespoons maple syrup or sugar of choice**
- **1 teaspoon vanilla extract**
- **3–5 tablespoons BōKU Super Cacao Nibs (to taste)**
- **Sliced bananas for serving (optional)**

How to BōKU

In a medium bowl, whisk together flour, baking powder, and salt. In a separate bowl mix together milk, oil, maple syrup, and vanilla extract. Next, pour your liquid mixture over the dry mixture and combine until only a few lumps remain. Fold in Super Cacao Nibs. Let sit for 5 minutes.

Lightly grease pan or electric skillet (preheated to 350°F). Scoop ¼ cup batter onto the hot skillet and cook for about 2 to 3 minutes, or until small bubbles form. Flip and cook the opposite side until light golden brown. Repeat with remaining batter, adjusting heat if necessary. Enjoy with organic maple syrup, sliced bananas if desired, and even more cacao nibs sprinkled on top!

Pumpkin Spice Protein Pancakes

We developed this seasonal recipe when we were moving into fall, as the pumpkin spice taste truly captures the essence of the season. Fall turned into winter, winter turned into spring, and we were still making the pancakes! For a taste that truly stands the test of all seasons, we recommend these pancakes as a scrumptious way to spice up your usual breakfast routine.

Prep time: 10 minutes   **Cook time**: 20 minutes   **Serves:** 3

- 1½ teaspoons ground flax
- 1½ tablespoons water
- ½ teaspoon apple cider vinegar
- ½ cup almond milk
- ¼ cup pumpkin purée
- ½ teaspoon vanilla extract
- ½–1 tablespoon coconut sugar
- ½ teaspoon cinnamon or pumpkin pie spice
- 1½ teaspoons baking powder
- ¼ teaspoon baking soda
- ¼ teaspoon sea salt
- 3 tablespoons (1 scoop) BōKU Super Protein
- ¾ cup rolled oats
- Agave nectar (or maple syrup) and pecans, for serving

How to BōKU

Put the flax and water in a blender and let sit for a minute or two to thicken. Next, add the remaining ingredients and blend until smooth. Let the batter sit for several minutes.

Meanwhile, heat a nonstick griddle (or large nonstick skillet) coated with cooking spray over medium heat. Spoon 2 heaping tablespoons batter per pancake on the griddle. Flip pancakes when tops are covered with bubbles and edges look cooked. Serve warm, topped with agave nectar or maple syrup and a sprinkle of pecans.

Super Cacao Muffins

As we're sure you know, muffins don't typically have the *best* reputation for being healthy. We didn't want to give up these timeless sweet treats, so we swapped out some ingredients for healthier ones—making this a delicious snack that you can enjoy without the guilt! The healthy fats of coconut oil, fiber of whole wheat flour, and antioxidants found in cacao nibs come together to make this muffin truly super!

Prep time: 5 minutes   **Cook time:** 25 minutes   **Serves:** 12

4 bananas

½ cup almond milk

1½ cups whole wheat flour

1½ teaspoon baking powder

½ cup coconut sugar

¼ cup extra-virgin olive oil or coconut oil

1 teaspoon vanilla extract

½ cup BōKU Super Cacao Nibs

How to BōKU

Preheat oven to 350°F and lightly grease a 12-cup muffin pan with coconut or extra-virgin olive oil.

In a blender, combine the bananas and almond milk until smooth. Set aside.

In a large bowl, combine the flour and baking powder. Add the banana mixture, coconut sugar, oil, and vanilla to the flour mixture and whisk to combine. Fold in the Super Cacao Nibs.

Scoop the batter into the muffin pan and bake for 20 or 25 minutes or until a toothpick inserted into the center comes out clean. Remove from the oven; allow muffins to cool at least 5 minutes before removing them from the pan. Place on a wire rack to cool completely.

Raw Super Oatmeal

Did you know that oatmeal is a superfood? It contains beta-glucan, which may help reduce cholesterol, plus unique antioxidants called avenanthramides! The beta-glucan in oatmeal is also known for stabilizing blood sugar, which can assist in keeping you feeling full until your next meal. Talk about a win-win! This is the perfect raw oatmeal recipe that's good for you in every way. Have it as an afternoon snack, or even as breakfast. It's easy to make and full of delicious natural ingredients.

Prep time: 8 minutes   **Serves:** 1

- 1 cup rolled oats, soaked overnight in amount of water suggested on package
- ¼ cup almond butter
- 1–2 tablespoons agave nectar
- ¼ cup unflavored almond milk, or more to reach desired consistency
- ¼ cup raisins
- ½ banana
- 2–3 tablespoons (2–3 scoops) BōKU Super Food
- ½ cup fresh or frozen fruit (fresh tastes better) of choice, such as blueberries, raspberries, peaches, or melon

How to BōKU

Place all ingredients in a food processor, blend to desired consistency, and enjoy!

Berry Delicious Breakfast Cookies

Your eyes do not deceive you. This cookie really is for *breakfast*. (Exciting, isn't it?) This fun and simple cookie has only five ingredients, one of which is the celebrated BōKU Super Berries blend, which is filled with antioxidants, vitamins, and minerals. The other ingredients also deserve mention: almond butter contains healthy fats, cranberries have antioxidants, and oats contain fiber.

Prep time: 5 minutes   **Cook time:** 15 minutes   **Makes:** 4 cookies

   1 cup rolled oats

   4 scoops (4 teaspoons) BōKU Super Berries

   ½ cup almond butter

   ½ cup brown sugar

   1 cup dried cranberries

   1–2 tablespoons melted coconut oil (only if needed)

How to BōKU

Preheat oven to 375°F. In a bowl, combine oats, Super Berries, almond butter, and brown sugar in a bowl and mix thoroughly. If your cookie dough is too dry, it could be because the almond butter did not contain enough oil (varies per brand); in this case, add 2 to 3 tablespoons melted coconut oil to moisten. Next, carefully fold in the cranberries and form dough into small balls (about 2 inches). Press the balls of dough slightly with your palm, place on a baking sheet, and bake for 12 to 15 minutes. Cookies will be slightly soft at first; make sure to let them sit for about 10 minutes or until firm before enjoying.

Super Berries Muffins

Crispy on top and moist in the middle, these tasty muffins are sure to impress even the pickiest of palates. Kick up the nutritional value with antioxidant-filled BōKU Super Berries and healthy fats from coconut oil, in addition to the fiber and minerals found in coconut sugar.

Prep time: 5 minutes   **Cook time:** 25 minutes   **Serves:** 12

> 4 bananas
>
> ½ cup almond milk
>
> 1½ cups whole wheat flour
>
> 1½ teaspoons baking powder
>
> 2 tablespoons (6 scoops) BōKU Super Berries
>
> ½ cup coconut sugar
>
> ¼ cup extra-virgin olive oil or melted coconut oil
>
> 1 teaspoon vanilla extract
>
> ½ cup fresh blueberries

How to BōKU

Preheat the oven to 350°F and lightly grease a 12-cup muffin pan with coconut or extra-virgin olive oil.

In a blender combine the bananas and almond milk until smooth. Set aside.

In a large bowl, combine the flour and baking powder. Add the banana mixture, Super Berries, sugar, oil, and vanilla, and whisk to combine. Fold in the blueberries.

Scoop batter into the muffin pan and bake for 20 or 25 minutes or until a toothpick inserted into the center comes out clean. Remove from the oven; make sure to allow the muffins to cool for at least 5 minutes before removing from the pan. Place them on a wire rack to cool completely.

Super Lunches & Dinners

Healthy Lunch Bowl with Avocado and Homemade Super Food Hummus

If you haven't yet fallen in love with hummus and all of the different ways to season and serve it, then grab your BōKU Super Food and your appetite for a quick and simple introduction on how to BōKU with this healthy and delish dish.

Prep time: 10 minutes   **Makes:** 2 cups hummus + toppings for 6–8 servings

Hummus

1 (15-ounce) can chickpeas, drained, liquid reserved

1 clove garlic, crushed

1 tablespoon (1 scoop) BōKU Super Food

2 teaspoons ground cumin

½ teaspoon salt

1 tablespoon olive oil

Salad

1½ cups fresh spinach leaves

6–8 cherry tomatoes

5–10 baby carrots

½ cucumber, sliced

½ avocado, sliced

½ cup canned chickpeas

3 tablespoons pumpkin seeds

How to BōKU

To make the hummus, in a blender or food processor, combine chickpeas, garlic, Super Food, cumin, salt, and olive oil. Blend on low speed, gradually adding reserved bean liquid until desired consistency is achieved.

To make the salad, place washed spinach in a medium-sized bowl. On top, arrange tomatoes, carrots, cucumber, avocado, and additional chickpeas. Dollop desired amount of fresh hummus atop for your dressing. Sprinkle pumpkin seeds on top for added flavor and nutrition.

Quick and Easy Avocado Sandwich

We think you'll really enjoy this simple yet delicious sandwich. Keep it basic, or easily add extra flavor by mixing in your favorite seasonings or applying your favorite spreads to the bread before you add the avocado. Try adding Italian herbs to the avocado or dashes of balsamic vinaigrette to the bread.

Prep time: 5 minutes   **Serves:** 1

- 2 slices of your favorite bread
- 1 ripe avocado
- 1 tablespoon (1 scoop) BōKU Super Food
- Salt and pepper to taste
- Cayenne pepper (optional)
- 4 slices tomato

How to BōKU

Toast bread if desired. Cut avocado in half and remove pit. Use a fork to scrape the flesh into a small bowl. Add the Super Food and salt and pepper to taste. Mix well with the fork, and for an extra kick, add a few pinches cayenne powder if desired.

Spread the avocado mixture on the bread with a butter knife. Top with tomato slices.

It's a Wrap!

This delicious wrap is made super with BōKU Homemade Super Food Hummus, but if you would like to kick it up a notch, mix in an additional half scoop of Super Food. Almost all veggies work great in wraps and can be substituted for any listed in the recipe, or a few more can be added—just be careful not to add too much so it is still manageable to wrap and eat!

Prep time: 10 minutes   **Serves:** 1

1 flatbread wrap

¼ cup Homemade Super Food Hummus (page 106)

2 medium leaves romaine lettuce

½ red bell pepper, thinly sliced

¼ cucumber, peeled and sliced

¼ red onion, thinly sliced

¼ lemon

How to BōKU

Place your wrap on an equal-sized piece of wax paper or a plate. Spread the Homemade Super Food Hummus evenly on the wrap leaving about an inch around the borders.

Place the romaine leaves with the ruffled edges hanging a little over the edge of the wrap. Evenly spread the veggies over the lettuce. Squeeze the lemon slice over the ingredients evenly, and roll up.

Veggie and Tofu Curry

Curry is known for its mix of abundantly flavorful spices, such as turmeric, fennel, coriander, cinnamon, and ginger. These spices cover a wide range of holistic health benefits and combine well with BōKU Super Food, making this slow-cooker dish an exotic, aromatic, and balanced mixture of sweet, spicy, and savory.

Prep time: 15 minute   **Cook time:** 20 minutes   **Serves:** 4–6

16 ounces extra-firm tofu, drained

2 tablespoons (2 scoops) BōKU Super Food

1 (14.5-ounce) can light coconut milk (or full fat)

1 cup vegetable broth

¼ cup Thai green or red curry paste

1 tablespoon fresh minced ginger

½ teaspoon turmeric

1 teaspoon salt

1 tablespoon coconut sugar

1 medium onion, chopped

1½ cups sliced bell pepper (frozen is okay)

¾ cup peas

1 small eggplant, chopped

Cooked brown rice or quinoa, for serving (optional)

How to BōKU

Place tofu in a tofu press and tighten knobs until snug. Put press on a plate or baking sheet to catch liquid, and press for 30 to 60 minutes, tightening knobs as needed. (If you don't have a tofu press, place tofu between paper towels or a kitchen towel. Place on plate and cover with heavy objects, like a couple books. Allow tofu to press for 30 to 60 minutes.)

Meanwhile, add Super Food, coconut milk, broth, curry paste, ginger, turmeric, salt, and coconut sugar to a slow cooker. Whisk until well combined. Add onion, bell pepper, peas, and eggplant, stirring to combine. Cook on high for 3 to 4 hours.

While the mixture is cooking, heat a large pan sprayed with olive oil over medium heat. Dice up the pressed tofu into bite-sized pieces. Cook tofu for a few minutes per side, or until golden. Set aside.

When curry has 30 minutes left to cook, add the cooked tofu. Allow curry and tofu to cook for the remaining 30 minutes and serve over brown rice or quinoa if desired.

Super Shroom Pho

Vietnamese cuisine hosts a lovely blend of spices, herbs, chiles, and unique dishes such as pho. This soup is full of vitality due to its flavorful broth, fresh veggies, BōKU Super Shrooms, and a variety of potent toppings such as basil, ginger, chiles, shiitake mushrooms, mung bean sprouts, and more. Try this recipe and other different international dishes that let you experience how delicious and nutritious eating around the world can be.

Prep time: 10 minutes   **Cook time:** 20 minutes   **Serves:** 4–6

2 cartons (8 cups) vegetable broth

6 green onions, thinly sliced

1 inch fresh ginger, peeled and grated

Salt to taste

2 tablespoons (2 scoops)
BōKU Super Shrooms

2 tablespoons butter

5 ounces shiitake mushrooms,
tough stems removed

1 tablespoon hoisin sauce,
plus more for serving

2 teaspoons sesame oil

1 (14-ounce) pack rice noodles,
cooked according to package instructions

2 cups bean sprouts

2 jalapeño peppers, thinly sliced

Fresh cilantro, basil, bean sprouts,
lime wedges, and Sriracha sauce for serving

How to BōKU

In a large saucepan, place the vegetable broth, green onions, ginger, and salt and bring to a boil. Reduce the heat and simmer for 15 minutes; then, turn off the heat and add the Super Shrooms.

While the broth is cooking, in a large pan, melt the butter over medium heat. Add the mushrooms and cook, stirring often, for about 5 minutes or until tender. Add the hoisin sauce and sesame oil and stir until it thickens and coats the mushrooms. Turn off the heat, and set aside.

Divide the cooked rice noodles among the serving bowls. Fill the bowls with the broth and top with the mushrooms. Top with cilantro, basil, bean sprouts, lime wedges, Sriracha sauce, and hoisin sauce.

Ratatouille BōKU

Ratatouille is a classic stew originating in the South of France, where eggplant, tomatoes, zucchini, sweet bell peppers, and onions grow in abundance. Complemented by the addition of BōKU Super Food, this dish is simple yet elegant, and many different subtle variations and techniques can help you make the recipe your own. Ultimately, ratatouille is a melody of the flavors of Provence: hearty homegrown vegetables stewed in ripe tomatoes and extra-virgin olive oil then topped off with Herbes de Provence and garlic.

Prep time: 45 minutes   **Cook time:** 4 hours + refrigerating overnight   **Serves:** 8

Purée

- 2 tablespoons olive oil
- 1 onion, roughly chopped
- 2 carrots, roughly chopped
- 2 celery stalks, roughly chopped
- 1 tablespoon chopped garlic
- 1 red bell pepper
- 1 anaheim pepper
- 2 tablespoons (2 scoops) BōKU Super Food
- 1 (28-ounce) can crushed tomatoes or 10–12 peeled Roma tomatoes, roughly chopped
- ½ cup basil leaves
- 1 teaspoon salt
- ½ teaspoon pepper
- 1 teaspoon Herbes de Provence

Vegetables

- 2 Japanese eggplants, thinly sliced
- 6 Roma tomatoes, thinly sliced
- 2 zucchini, thinly sliced
- 2 yellow squash, thinly sliced
- Salt and pepper

Topping

- 2 tablespoons extra-virgin olive oil
- 2 cloves garlic, minced
- 1 tablespoon fresh thyme leaves, chopped (or ¾ teaspoon dried)

How to BōKU

For the purée, in a large pan, heat the oil over medium heat. Once the oil is hot, add the onion, carrot, celery, and garlic. Cook until all ingredients are softened and a fork easily pierces the carrots.

Meanwhile, blacken the skin of both peppers on all sides, either under the broiler or over an open flame on the stovetop. Place the blackened peppers in a bowl covered tightly with plastic wrap or in a resealable bag to cool. Once the peppers are cool enough to handle, peel the skins.

Place the Super Food, sautéed vegetables, peeled peppers, tomatoes, basil, salt, pepper, and Herbes de Provence in a blender and purée until smooth. Spread the purée on the bottom of an oven-safe pan or skillet and layer the sliced eggplant, tomatoes, and squash on top of the sauce in a circular formation, starting from the outside and working in. Season with salt and pepper.

For the topping, mix together the oil, garlic, and thyme and drizzle over the veggies.

Reduce the oven temperature to 275°F, cover the pan with foil, and bake for 3 hours. Refrigerate overnight to let the flavors mingle and the veggies marinate.

To serve, place the uncovered pan in a 350°F oven and bake for 45 minutes if cold, and 20 minutes if already warm/hot.

Spaghetti Squash Pasta

Now this is no ordinary gourd! Spaghetti squash's claim to fame (and reason for it's name) is that it shreds into spaghetti-like strands after being baked. It's uncanny how similar the squash strands and real spaghetti look, but don't be fooled: the flavors are completely different. This recipe is relatively easy to make and is a great way to start exploring the possibilities of cooking with spaghetti squash. Plus, you can boost the beneficial properties of this dish simply by adding BōKU Super Shrooms to the sauce. Who knows what's next? BōKU Super Food and spaghetti squash lasagna, anyone?

Prep time: 15 minutes   **Cook time:** 40–45 minutes   **Serves:** 2

    1 large spaghetti squash

    2 tablespoons olive oil

    ¾ teaspoon salt

    ¼ teaspoon pepper

    1 (24-ounce jar) your favorite pasta sauce (or homemade!)

    Parmesan or vegan cheese for garnish (optional)

How to BōKU

Preheat oven to 375°F. Halve squash lengthwise, and use a spoon to scoop out and discard seeds from the middle of each half. Arrange squash in a 9x13-inch casserole dish, cut sides up. Drizzle olive oil inside each half, and season with salt and pepper. Bake for 40 to 45 minutes or until soft. When done, rake a fork back and forth across the squash to remove its flesh in strands, until it looks just like spaghetti! Serve with your favorite pasta sauce. Use basil as garnish. Add regular or vegan parmesan if desired.

BōKU Super Burger

Here's an ode to the nostalgic summer BBQ memory of biting into a juicy burger with all the fixings. We have created this juicy meat-free rendition that will have your taste buds salivating with anticipation, just like that summer meal. With BōKU Super Food added to the mix, these patties will be packed with essential vitamins, minerals, digestive enzymes, and phytonutrients to make you the super person you are; plus, the plant-based proteins from quinoa and black beans will make you savor every bite of your homemade BōKU Super Burger.

Prep time: 15 minutes   **Cook time:** 50 minutes   **Makes:** 8 patties

½ cup quinoa

1 small onion, finely chopped (1 cup)

6 oil-packed sun-dried tomatoes, drained and finely chopped (about ¼ cup)

1½ cups cooked black beans or 1 (15-ounce) can black beans,
    rinsed and drained, divided

2 cloves garlic, minced (2 teaspoons)

2 teaspoons dried steak seasoning

2 scoops (2 tablespoons) BōKU Super Food

8 whole-grain hamburger buns

How to BōKU

Stir together quinoa and 1½ cups water in small saucepan, and season with salt, if desired. Bring to a boil. Cover, reduce heat to medium-low, and simmer 20 minutes, or until all liquid is absorbed. (This will give you 1½ cups cooked quinoa.)

Meanwhile, place onion and sun-dried tomatoes in medium nonstick skillet, and cook over medium heat. (The oil left on the tomatoes should be enough to sauté the onion.) Cook 3 to 4 minutes, or until onion has softened. Stir in ¾ cup black beans, garlic, steak seasoning, and 1½ cups water. Simmer 10 to 12 minutes, or until most of liquid has evaporated.

Transfer bean-onion mixture to food processor, add ¾ cup cooked quinoa, and process until smooth. Transfer to bowl, and stir in remaining ¾ cup quinoa and remaining ¾ cup black beans. Season with salt and pepper, if desired, and let cool.

Preheat oven to 350°F, and generously coat baking sheet with cooking spray. Shape bean mixture into 8 patties (½ cup each), and place on prepared baking sheet. Bake 20 minutes, or until patties are crisp on top. Flip patties with spatula, and bake 10 more minutes, or until both sides are crisp and brown. Serve on buns with all of your favorite toppings! We love to use romaine lettuce, tomatoes, and red onion.

Almond-Sesame Noodles

This exciting and exotic noodle dish is sure to tickle your taste buds as well as add a major nutritive boost to your meal. Our peppy Almond-Sesame Noodles include BōKU Super Food, which adds a whopping 50-plus functional superfoods to your plate in just a single scoop! The ginger in this recipe was chosen for its history of use in forms of traditional/alternative medicine as well as for its defining and unique taste. The almond butter, which has naturally occurring healthy unsaturated fats, balances this zesty sauce out with its smooth taste.

Prep time: 25 minutes   **Serves:** 4–6

2 large cloves garlic, peeled

1 1-inch piece fresh ginger, peeled

2 scallions, white and green portions, cut into 2-inch pieces

¼ cup fresh cilantro

1 cup raw almond butter

¼ cup tamari

Zest and juice from 1 lime

2 tablespoons maple syrup

1 tablespoon white miso

1 teaspoon Sriracha sauce

3 tablespoons (3 scoops) BōKU Super Food

2 tablespoons dark sesame oil

Warm water, brewed green tea, or chicken stock for thinning sauce

Sea salt to taste, if needed

1 pound your favorite pasta noodles

Slivered almonds and sesame seeds for serving (optional)

How to BōKU

To make the sauce, in a food processor fitted with the metal blade, run the processor and drop in the garlic, ginger, scallions, and cilantro through the feed tube; process to mince. Add almond butter, tamari, lime zest and juice, miso, Sriracha, and Super Food, and process until smooth, stopping to scrape sides as needed. Add in the sesame oil and process until incorporated. Add in warm water, tea, or chicken stock by the tablespoonful until you reach the desired consistency (it should be thick). Check for seasoning.

To make the noodles, place a large pot filled with water on high heat. Add a heaping teaspoon of salt to the water. Once the water comes to a boil, add pasta and reduce heat to medium-high. Cook as directed on the label; then drain when ready. Rinse the cooked pasta with cold water to stop the cooking. Toss with sauce when ready to serve. Garnish with slivered almonds and sesame seeds if desired.

Lentil Super Soup

Lentil Super Soup is a simple, filling, and yummy dish full of beneficial nutrients like fiber, vitamins, protein, and minerals; it's also low in fat and calories. It's a healthy and warm complete meal in a bowl, especially when you stir a little BōKU Super Food and Super Shrooms into the pot to make a super soup fit for a super person like yourself!

Prep time: 10 minutes   **Cook time:** 35 minutes   **Serves:** 2

1 tablespoon olive oil	1¼ cups lentils (any color except red), rinsed
1 medium celery stalk, diced	1 bay leaf
1 medium carrot, peeled and diced	¼ teaspoon finely chopped fresh thyme leaves
½ medium yellow onion, diced	1 tablespoon (1 scoop) BōKU Super Food
3 medium garlic cloves, minced	1 teaspoon (1 scoop) BōKU Super Shrooms
Salt and freshly ground black pepper	1 teaspoon red wine or sherry vinegar
1 quart low-sodium vegetable broth	2 ounces spinach leaves (about ½ bunch)
1 (15-ounce) can diced tomatoes with their juices	

How to BōKU

Heat the oil in a large saucepan over medium heat until shimmering, about 3 minutes. Add the celery, carrot, and onion and cook, stirring occasionally, until the vegetables have softened, about 10 minutes. Stir in the garlic and cook until fragrant, about 1 minute. Season with several generous pinches of salt and pepper. Add the broth, tomatoes with their juices, lentils, bay leaf, and thyme and stir to combine. Then stir in the BōKU Super Food and Super Shrooms. Cover and bring to a simmer, about 15 minutes. Once simmering, reduce the heat to low and continue simmering, covered, until the lentils and vegetables are soft, about 15 minutes more.

Taste and season with more salt or pepper as needed, then stir in the vinegar. Add the spinach and stir until wilted. If you prefer a creamier texture, purée half of the soup in a blender and add it back to the pot. Remove bay leaf before serving.

Healthy Desserts

RAWsome Strawberry "Cheesecake"

Say CHEESE . . . cake! Raw, vegan, cheesecake, that is. This delectable treat uses cashews instead of the usual cream-cheese filling found in cheesecake, which gives this treat a nutritional punch that your typical cheesecake cannot claim. RAWsome Strawberry "Cheesecake" contains antioxidants, heart-protective monounsaturated fats, along with magnesium, manganese, phosphorus, and zinc! Don't forget the topping, a delicious purée of strawberries and BōKU Super Berries, which is also brimming with vitamins and antioxidants. It truly makes this dessert something worth talking about!

Prep time: 35 minutes + 4 hours in freezer to set   **Makes:** One 9-inch cake

Cake

    1½ cups Medjool dates, pitted

    1½ cups raw almonds

    2 lemons, juiced, about ½ cup

    ⅔ cup melted coconut oil

    1¼ cups full-fat coconut milk

    1 cup agave nectar

    2 teaspoons (2 scoops) BōKU Super Berries

    3 cups raw cashew pieces, soaked overnight, then drained

    1 vanilla bean

Topping

    2 cups strawberries, tops removed

    1 tablespoon agave nectar

    4 teaspoons (4 scoops) BōKU Super Berries

How to BōKU

To make the crust, soak the dates in warm water for about 10 minutes; drain. Pulse dates in a food processor until they form a thick paste; transfer to a bowl. Add almonds to same food processor bowl (no need to clean in between!) and pulse until finely chopped. Add the date paste back into the food processor and pulse together with the almonds until the mixture forms a ball. Press the mixture firmly and evenly into the bottom of a 9-inch round pan and place in the freezer while you move on to the filling.

To make the filling, combine lemon juice, coconut oil, coconut milk, agave nectar, Super Berries, and cashews in a blender. Start on low speed; then gradually increase to the highest speed. Blend until it is extremely smooth, with no chunks of nuts visible! Next, scrape the seeds from your vanilla bean into the blender and blend on low speed until the seeds have been evenly distributed throughout the filling mixture. Pour the filling onto the crust in the pan and return it to the freezer while you make the fruit purée topping.

To make the fruit purée topping, in a clean food processor bowl, combine strawberries, remaining 1 tablespoon agave nectar, and Super Berries and blend until smooth. Pour over the top of the cashew-cream layer of the cheesecake, gently smoothing it out with a spatula. Freeze at least 4 hours or until solid. Let stand 10 minutes at room temperature before slicing and serving.

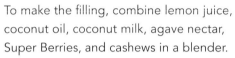

Raw Chocolate Banana Pudding

This easy-to-make pudding is sure to be a hit with kids and adults alike. Start with avocado, which gives this raw pudding a velvety soft finish and nourishes your body with healthy fats. Next, dial in the sweet and balanced taste with cocoa powder and bananas; then kick the nutrient power into overdrive with a super boost of Super Food.

Prep time: 5 minutes + 1 hour in refrigerator
Serves: 2

> 1 ripe avocado
>
> 4 ripe bananas (the riper, the better!)
>
> ¼ cup unsweetened cocoa powder
>
> 1 tablespoon (1 scoop) BōKU Super Food
>
> Sliced banana and cashews for garnish (optional)

How to BōKU

Scoop out avocado into a blender. Add in peeled bananas, cocoa powder, and Super Food and blend on high until smooth. Pour contents into a bowl and chill for an hour to thicken and allow flavors to meld. Serve as is or top with sliced banana and cashews if desired.

Vegan Super Custard

We originally created this custard for Halloween to provide a ghoulish-looking dessert that would be fun for parents and kids to make and enjoy together. We liked how it turned out so much, we decided to bring it into our main collection of Super Food recipes! Brimming with phytonutrients from Super Food and protein from the silken tofu, we hope you will love this delicious custard as much as we do.

Prep time: 10 minutes + 1 hour in refrigerator   **Makes:** 2 cups

12 ounces silken tofu, room temperature

⅓ teaspoon pink salt (or substitute regular salt)

½–1 teaspoon vanilla bean powder or 1 vanilla bean, seeds scraped

⅛ teaspoon cinnamon

3 tablespoons extra-virgin coconut oil, melted

¼–½ cup grade B maple syrup (to taste)

1 tablespoon (1 scoop) BōKU Super Food

BōKU Super Cacao Nibs for garnish

How to BōKU

Add the tofu, salt, vanilla bean powder, cinnamon, and melted coconut oil to a blender. Blend on low until smooth. Add in ¼ cup maple syrup and blend until smooth. Taste and add more sweetener as desired. (We added about ⅓ cup total.) Blend for another 1 to 3 minutes on medium to whip some air into the mixture. Add Super Food and mix again until fully blended.

Pour mixture evenly into clear glass cups. (Clear plastic will also work if you don't have glass.) Place in the refrigerator until fully chilled, at least an hour for the richest texture. For a softer, more melted texture, you can serve only slightly chilled. Just before serving, sprinkle with Super Cacao Nibs.

Orange Protein Pops

Every blazing hot day warrants an icy treat to cool you off. These pops are sweetly simple to create: all you need is a popsicle mold and a freezer! The orange juice in this recipe delivers a tangy kick while the almond milk softens the flavor for a creamy finish. Guilt free with only naturally occurring sugars and highly absorbable protein, these will quickly become a warm-weather favorite.

Prep time: 5 minutes + 4 hours in freezer   **Makes:** 4

- ½ cup fresh squeezed orange juice
- ½ cup almond milk
- 1 teaspoon vanilla extract
- 3 tablespoons (1 scoop) BōKU Super Protein

How to BōKU

Blend all ingredients together. Divide mixture evenly among 4 popsicle molds; place in the freezer for about 4 hours or until completely frozen.

BōKU Bonbons

Bonbons never tasted so good (or packed such a nutritious punch!). Try this sweet, coconut-covered, delectable chocolate treat and feel good about your choice while you indulge.

Prep time: 10 minutes   **Makes:** about 2 dozen

- 2 cups raw, unsalted macadamia nuts
- ¼ teaspoon fine sea salt
- 15 Medjool dates, pitted
- ⅓ cup unsweetened cocoa powder
- ¼ cup (about 4 scoops) BōKU Super Food
- ¼ teaspoon ground cardamom
- ½ teaspoon cinnamon
- 1 tablespoon raw honey or agave nectar
- 1 teaspoon vanilla extract
- ¼ cup finely chopped candied ginger (dried apricots or golden raisins are good, too)
- ½ cup shredded unsweetened coconut, additional cocoa powder, or sesame seeds for coating

How to BōKU

In a food processor fitted with the steel blade, process the nuts with the salt until finely chopped, taking care not to process to a paste. Add the dates and process to combine well. Add the cocoa powder, Super Food, cardamom, cinnamon, honey or agave, and vanilla. Process until mixture is uniform in texture. Add the ginger and pulse until just combined (it's nice to leave the ginger in pieces for texture). Turn mixture out into a bowl. Form small bonbons (1 to 2 tablespoons each) by squeezing and rolling the mixture between your palms. Roll bonbons in the coconut, cocoa, or sesame seeds to coat. Bonbons keep well for 1 week refrigerated (they taste great cold!), or freeze up to 3 months.

Super Matcha Scones

Steeped in Japanese tradition, our Super Matcha Green Tea blend is one of the world's most potent natural sources of antioxidants, immune-boosting flavonols, and catechins (EGCg). We select only the finest organic Japanese ceremonial and traditional whole leaf matcha powdered green tea to form our proprietary blend. The result is a regal, full-bodied, richly organic, and balanced experience. Here we combine Super Matcha Green Tea with a decadent blueberry scone, delivering zen-like energy to keep you focused on the go or feeling good going with the flow.

Prep time: 15 minutes   Bake time: 15 minutes   Makes: 6

- 2 cups all-purpose gluten-free flour, plus extra for sprinkling
- 2 teaspoons baking powder
- 1 tablespoon BōKU Super Matcha Green Tea
- ½ teaspoon baking soda
- ½ teaspoon xanthan gum
- ⅛ teaspoon salt

- ¼ cup coconut oil, melted
- 1 teaspoon vanilla extract
- 1 teaspoon maple syrup
- ¼ cup non-dairy milk
- ½ cup blueberries

How to BōKU

Preheat oven to 400°F and grease a baking sheet. In a large bowl, whisk together flour, powder, Super Matcha Green Tea, baking soda, xanthan gum, and salt. In a small bowl or cup, mix together coconut oil, vanilla, maple syrup, and milk. Pour wet ingredients into flour mixture, stirring until thoroughly combined. Use your hands to knead dough. If batter is too dry to knead into a ball, add 1 to 2 more tablespoons of milk. Fold in blueberries.

Sprinkle flour on a clean surface. Form batter into ball and flatten into a 2-inch-thick circle. Use a sharp knife to slice dough into 6 triangles (3 cuts across). Place pieces on baking sheet.

Bake for 15 minutes, or until edges are golden brown. Remove from oven and let cool for at least 15 minutes before serving.

Vegan Raw Matcha Lemon Biscotti

This recipe is a new way to have one of those comforting morning treats without any of the guilt. Featuring Super Matcha Green Tea paired with zesty fresh lemon, these biscotti are sure to be a refreshing energizer for the productive day ahead.

Prep time: 45 minutes + 13–17 hours drying time

Makes: 10–12

1½ cups whole raw almonds, soaked in water for 1 hour and drained

Zest of 1 lemon

3 tablespoons freshly squeezed lemon juice

¼ cup filtered water

3 tablespoons raw agave nectar

1 teaspoon BōKU Super Matcha Green Tea

¼ cup ground flaxseeds

1 tablespoon raw vanilla extract or regular organic vanilla extract

½ teaspoon fine sea salt

How to BōKU

In a food processor fitted with the metal S-blade, add the soaked almonds, lemon zest, lemon juice, water, and agave, and process until smooth, about 2 to 3 minutes, scraping the sides when necessary. Next, add the Super Matcha Green Tea, flaxseeds, vanilla, and salt. Process until you have a smooth consistency.

Separate the dough into fourths. Make each piece 5 inches long by 3 inches wide by 1 inch tall and place on a dehydrator sheet tray at least 1 or 2 inches apart. Dry at 105°F for 9 to 12 hours.

Cut pieces into individual biscotti and place cut-side down on the mesh sheets. Dry for 4 to 5 hours or until crispy. Share them right away or store in an airtight container for up to 2 weeks.

BōKU Tip

If you do not want to use a dehydrator, set your oven to the lowest temperature (150°F–250°F), form the squares on a lightly oiled parchment paper–lined cookie sheet, and put them in the oven for 2 to 3 hours, or until firm. Then, slice and bake biscotti for another 3 to 4 hours or until crisp and slightly golden brown. They will not be raw at this point, but most of the nutrients will not be harmed in the process. If desired, you may want to press slivered almonds into the biscotti prior to firming up.

Vegan Zucchini Bread

Sugar, spice, and everything nice. Any time of year can feel like baking season with this moist zucchini bread sprinkled with cacao nibs—known as the "food of the gods" to ancient civilizations. This divine recipe is comprised of ingredients that are wonderful tasting and wonderful for you! To name a few, ground zucchini, ginger, cinnamon, and coconut oil supply your body with antioxidants, healthy fats, and revitalizing nutrients to help you thrive throughout the day.

Prep time: 50–60 minutes   **Cook time:** 50–60 minutes   **Serves:** 16 (1 loaf)

1½ cups whole wheat flour (or your favorite gluten-free flour)

1 teaspoon baking powder

½ teaspoon baking soda

¼ teaspoon fine sea salt

¼ teaspoon ground ginger

2 teaspoons ground cinnamon

1 teaspoon apple cider vinegar

½ cup unsweetened soy milk or almond milk

½ cup organic evaporated cane sugar

¼ cup unsweetened applesauce

¼ cup virgin coconut oil, melted

1 cup finely shredded zucchini

1½ teaspoons pure vanilla extract

½ cup toasted walnuts or pecans, chopped

2 tablespoons BōKU Super Cacao Nibs

How to BōKU

Preheat oven to 350°F. Spray bottom of an 8x4-inch loaf pan with cooking spray (we prefer to use coconut oil spray!).

Mix together flour, baking powder, baking soda, salt, ginger, and cinnamon in a large bowl. Set aside.

Stir together the vinegar and milk; let stand for 2 minutes or until thickened. In a medium bowl, thoroughly mix together milk mixture, sugar, applesauce, coconut oil, zucchini, and vanilla until well blended. Add flour mixture, stirring only until combined. Stir in nuts and Cacao Nibs. Spread batter evenly in pan.

Bake 50 to 60 minutes or until bread is golden brown and passes the toothpick test! (Stick a toothpick in the middle of the bread; if it comes out clean, it's done.) Cool in pan for 10 minutes. Then, remove from pan and cool completely on a wire rack.

Raw MACAroon

Craving something sweet? Look no further than this Raw MACAroon recipe. These vegan cookies are a delicious nutritional treat you won't even have to wait for "cheat day" to indulge in! Step into taste-bud bliss all while getting your omega-3's, protein, and fiber—plus all the benefits of BōKU Super Maca!

Prep time: 10 minutes   **Cook time:** Refrigerate until desired consistency is reached

Serves: 30 1-inch balls or 10 cookies

- 1 cup slivered almonds
- ½ cup soft dates, pitted
- 2 tablespoons BōKU Super Maca
- ¼ cup ground flaxseeds
- 3 tablespoons maple syrup
- Pinch sea salt
- 2 cups unsweetened shredded coconut

How to BōKU

In your food processor, add all ingredients except the shredded coconut. Blend until close to dough-like consistency. Add coconut slowly, pulsing the food processor, until fully mixed. (Test to make sure the dough sticks together. If not, just add more dates or maple syrup!)

Use a small scoop (melon baller or teaspoon) to make small balls, or press dough into a muffin tin or favorite cookie mold! Refrigerate immediately, allowing the MACAroons to "set" until they reach your desired consistency.

Matcha Nice Cream

I scream, you scream, we all scream for nice cream! This frozen little wonder is easier to make than you'd think. Plus, you'll be reaping the many benefits of Super Matcha Green Tea, such as energy and antioxidants, all while satisfying your sweet tooth!

Prep time: 4–6 hours   **Serves:** 4–6

- 1 cup raw cashews, soaked 4–6 hours and rinsed well
- 2 cups full-fat coconut milk, chilled and divided from water
- 2–3 tablespoons BōKU Super Matcha Green Tea
- ¾ cup organic white, gold, or raw sugar or maple syrup
- 1 teaspoon vanilla extract
- ½ cup almond milk
- Pinch salt
- Mint leaves for garnish (optional)

How to BōKU

In a blender, combine cashews and coconut milk until the mixture is thick and creamy.

Add remaining ingredients and blend until creamy. Place mixture in an airtight container and freeze for 1 hour. Then, stir, and freeze for another hour or until it hardens completely. Garnish with mint leaves if desired and serve.

Baked Apples with Super Fuel Crumble

They say an apple a day keeps the doctor away. If that is true, we can only image what this nutrition-packed baked apple dish can do! Cinnamon, which has been prized for its medicinal properties for thousands of years, gives the apples a dessert-like taste and provides antioxidants. Super Fuel plays a wonderful role by delivering a chocolatey flavor derived from organic fair-trade cocoa. But it doesn't just stop at taste: Super Fuel also provides super adaptors such as cordyceps, reishi, and marshmallow root, all known to be beneficial for optimal vitality and resilience. This recipe is truly delicious and makes a perfect dessert or even a healthy snack.

Prep time: 10 minutes   **Cook time:** 50 minutes   **Serves:** 4

2 apples (Gala apples work well, but choose a local variety if available), halved and cored

1 teaspoon cinnamon

¼ cup pecans and almonds, chopped

½ cup organic rolled oats

1 teaspoon cinnamon

1 tablespoon coconut oil, melted

1 tablespoon maple syrup

1 tablespoon ground chia seeds

1 tablespoon (1 scoop) BōKU Super Fuel

1 teaspoon vanilla extract

1 tablespoon water

Pinch salt

How to BōKU

Preheat oven to 375°F. Line a baking sheet with parchment paper or foil. Place the apple halves on the baking sheet and sprinkle each half with ¼ teaspoon cinnamon. In a small bowl, combine remaining ingredients.

Pack each apple half with one-quarter of the oat mixture. Bake for 30 to 40 minutes or until apples are tender. Allow to cool for 5 minutes before serving.

Vegan Matcha Donuts

Have your tea and eat it, too! These delicious vegan, organic matcha green tea donuts will satisfy your sweet tooth and give you a boost of antioxidants and energy. The energy from matcha is really special: the amino acid L-Theanine found in the tea leaves has a calming effect on the body that helps to balance out the caffeine. Feel great enjoying these benefits in this yummy baked, not fried, treat!

Prep time: 18 minutes   **Cook time:** 12 minutes   **Makes:** 6 (depending on size of molds)

Donuts

  1½ cups whole wheat flour

  2 tablespoons sugar

  2 teaspoons baking powder

  ¼ teaspoon salt

  ¼ teaspoon cinnamon

  ¾ cup almond milk

  1 teaspoon raw apple cider vinegar

  1 teaspoon vanilla extract

  ¼ cup unsweetened applesauce

  ¼ cup organic coconut oil, plus more for greasing pan

Glaze

  1 cup icing sugar

  1 teaspoon BōKU Super Matcha Green Tea

  3 tablespoons almond milk

  Sprinkles or organic coconut sprinkles (for garnish)

How to BōKU

Preheat oven to 350°F and grease a donut pan with coconut oil.

To make the donuts, combine flour, sugar, baking powder, salt, and cinnamon in a large bowl. In a medium bowl, combine almond milk, vinegar, vanilla, applesauce, and coconut oil. Add the wet ingredients to the dry ingredients, and mix until just combined and a soft dough is formed.

Scoop dough into the prepared donut pan and bake for 12 minutes. Remove from the oven and allow to cool.

To make your glaze, mix together the icing sugar, Super Matcha Green Tea, and almond milk.

Once the donuts have cooled, simply dip each donut into the bowl of icing, and set on a cooling rack. Top with sprinkles or organic coconut sprinkles. Serve at room temperature and store leftovers in an airtight container.

Vegan Gluten-Free Choco-Banana Protein Bars

These easy-to-make protein bars are amazing for any time of the day. Eat one before the gym for an uplifting pre-workout snack, munch on one at work, or try packing them in your little one's lunchbox for a tasty treat the other kids will be begging to trade their snacks for! The Super Protein in these bars is readily absorbable. Super Cacao Nibs deliver magnesium, a theobromine buzz to wake you up, and tryptophan to make you feel happy! All this is nestled in a winning combination of banana and chocolate; this bar is sure to be a hit all around!

Prep time: 10 minutes　　**Cook time:** 15 minutes　　**Serves:** 16

- 1 cup gluten-free oats
- ½ cup (8 scoops) BōKU Super Protein
- ½ cup unsweetened cocoa powder
- ½ teaspoon baking powder
- ½ teaspoon baking soda
- 3 medium to large ripe bananas

- 1 teaspoon vanilla extract
- ¼ cup raw honey
- ⅓ cup BōKU Super Cacao Nibs
- 2 tablespoons chocolate chips for garnish (optional)

How to BōKU
Preheat oven to 350°F.

Make oat flour by placing oats in a food processor and blending until oats resemble flour.

In a medium bowl, stir together oat flour, Super Protein, cocoa powder, baking powder, and baking soda.

Place banana, vanilla, and honey in blender for 1 to 2 minutes or until smooth and creamy; add to flour mixture. Fold in Cacao Nibs, pour batter into pan, and bake for 15 minutes or until knife inserted in center of bars comes out clean. Cool on a wire rack for 10 to 15 minutes.

If desired, melt chocolate chips and drizzle over bars. Cut into 16 squares and enjoy!

Chocolate Coconut Energy Bites

Dessert-like treats with zero guilt, anyone? These energy bites have the rich texture and delectable taste to make you feel like you slipped up on your healthy eating plan, but really, you didn't even come close! Made with all whole foods, including dates—which are a good source of dietary fiber, antioxidants, and the essential minerals potassium and magnesium—along with metabolism-supporting Super Matcha Green Tea, this recipe is a winner with every bite.

Prep time: 15 minutes   **Serves:** Makes 10 1-inch balls

- ½ cup soft dates, pitted
- ½ cup raw almonds
- ¼ cup unsweetened cocoa powder
- 1 tablespoon BōKU Super Matcha Green Tea
- 1 tablespoon unsweetened almond milk
- 1 cup BōKU Toasted Coconut Chips (or unsweetened coconut shavings)

How to BōKU

Add dates and almonds to the bowl of a food processor, and blend until the ingredients turn into a sticky ball. Break up the mixture and add the cocoa powder, Super Matcha Green Tea, and almond milk. Blend until all ingredients have been combined and turn into a sticky, dough-like ball. Roll the mixture into 10 small balls with your hands. Roll each ball in coconut shavings until fully covered with coconut. Place on sheet of parchment paper. Store in refrigerator for up to 2 weeks or longer in freezer.

Super Cacao Cookies

Calling all chocolate chip cookie lovers: this recipe is for you! We've swapped out regular chocolate chips for Super Cacao Nibs, a healthy (and delicious) alternative to chocolate chips with amazing health benefits. Properties of Super Cacao Nibs are even thought to stimulate the brain, triggering feel good hormones and endorphins! Hip-hip-hooray!

Prep: 5 minutes   **Cook:** 10 minutes   **Makes:** 10–12 cookies

> 1 cup softened soy margarine
>
> ½ cup brown sugar
>
> ½ cup white sugar
>
> ¼ cup soy milk
>
> 1 teaspoon vanilla extract
>
> 2¼ cups all-purpose flour
>
> 1 teaspoon baking soda
>
> ½ teaspoon salt
>
> 1 cup BōKU Super Cacao Nibs

How to BōKU

Preheat oven to 350°F and line a baking sheet with parchment paper.

In a mixing bowl, blend together the margarine, brown sugar, and white sugar. Then add the soy milk and vanilla and mix well until it is nice and creamy. Next, add the flour, baking soda, and salt, and mix with a wooden spoon or hand mixer. Finally, fold in the Super Cacao Nibs. (If you really love that chocolatey taste, feel free to toss a few more in!)

Drop the dough by tablespoons onto the baking sheet, making sure that cookies are spaced a few inches apart. Bake for 8 to 10 minutes or until the edges are brown.

Matcha and White Chocolate Strawberries

This is not your average chocolate-covered strawberry. This delectable, sweet, and juicy delight is a perfect balance of fruit, white chocolate, and Super Matcha Green Tea. Just because this matcha happens to be nestled in delicious white chocolate doesn't mean you can't still reap the nutritional benefits! Enjoy this treat knowing it contains antioxidants and minerals to help you thrive and live your best life.

Prep time: 10 minutes   **Cook:** 10–15 minutes   **Makes:** 12 strawberries

- **12 large strawberries**
- **½ cup white chocolate**
- **½ teaspoons (or more to taste) BōKU Super Matcha Green Tea**

How to BōKU

In a small saucepan, melt white chocolate over medium heat, stirring occasionally until fully melted. Then, stir in Super Matcha Green Tea and remove from heat. To avoid burning yourself, we recommend transferring your chocolate mixture into a medium-sized bowl. Next, dip your strawberries in the mixture one by one, allowing the excess to drip back in the bowl. Place on waxed paper and let harden at room temperature, about 10 to15 minutes. To speed up this process, you may place finished strawberries in the refrigerator for 5 minutes.

Red, White, and Blue Nice Cream

Celebrate a new independence from feeling guilty about ice cream with BōKU's protein- and antioxidant-rich Red, White, and Blue Nice Cream! This dish is super simple to make, low in fat, and contains only naturally occurring sugars that your body can recognize and digest. The combination of Super Berries, sliced strawberries, and blueberries creates an antioxidant powerhouse that you've never seen in any ice cream before!

Prep time: 8 minutes + additional time to freeze bananas   **Serves:** 4–6

- 5–6 bananas, peeled and frozen in a plastic bag

- 3 tablespoons (1 scoop) BōKU Triple-Source Vegan Protein, plus 3 tablespoons (1 scoop) to sprinkle on top

- 4 teaspoons (4 scoops) BōKU Super Berries, plus 2 teaspoons (2 scoops) to sprinkle on top

- ½ cup non-dairy milk (such as almond milk)

- 2–3 strawberries, sliced

- ¼ cup fresh blueberries

How to BōKU

Chop frozen bananas and place them in a blender. Add the Triple-Source Vegan Protein, Super Berries, and non-dairy milk and blend until thick and creamy. Use an ice cream scoop or spoon and place 3 scoops per serving in bowls. Place the sliced strawberries on the left side of the scoops, sprinkle Super Berries on the right next to the strawberry slices, and sprinkle Super Protein on the right of the Super Berries. Place the fresh blueberries on the right of the scoops to create the red, white, and blue sequence.

Index